Twayne's United States Authors Series

Sylvia E. Bowman, *Editor*

INDIANA UNIVERSITY

John Burroughs

JOHN BURROUGHS

By PERRY D. WESTBROOK

State University of New York-Albany

 227

Twayne Publishers, Inc.   ::   New York

ISBN 0-8057-0117-6
MANUFACTURED IN THE UNITED STATES OF AMERICA

To Tenpa and Joyce

Preface

The writing career of John Burroughs extended from 1860 to 1921. A contributor to most of the magazines of importance in America during this period, he wrote a sufficient number of essays to fill the twenty-three volumes of his collected works, which by no means include his complete output. With the exception of some poetry, nearly all of it mediocre, Burroughs confined himself to the essay, a genre in which he developed great skill. For the most part, his writings fall into four main categories as to subject matter: studies and descriptions of outdoor nature; discussions of philosophy, including speculations on science and theology; accounts of travel; and literary criticism. This book attempts to describe and assess Burroughs' contributions in each of these areas; but closest attention is given to his work in criticism and philosophy. This portion of his writing is commonly slighted in favor of his nature pieces, which doubtless deserve the high and continuing praise they have received but which should not be permitted to eclipse the remaining two-thirds or three-quarters of his output.

It is regrettable that demands of organization necessitate the categorizing of Burroughs' works at all; for, as will be seen, there is a singleness of purpose and outlook that pervades all his writing on whatever subject. To devote, as I have done, a chapter to Burroughs the literary critic, another to Burroughs the nature writer, a third to him as a philosopher, and so forth, is artificial—however unavoidable—because to an almost unique degree he exemplifies the Emersonian concept of a *man* writing rather than the author-specialist that Emerson deplored. Indeed Burroughs filled many roles other than that of author; he was a serious and successful farmer, a bank examiner, an ornithologist, as well as a scholar and a meditator on all that he saw, read, and did. He could build a house, chop and split firewood, or lay up a stone wall as effectively as he could compose an essay. He saw life as a unity; and his own life was a unity.

Except in presenting Burroughs' boyhood and youth, I have had to avoid, as unmanageable, a strictly chronological approach to his life and works. At all times in his productive years Burroughs was engaged in his usual diversity of activities and in writing on a wide range of subjects. An attempt like that of Norman Foerster in *Nature in American Literature* to divide Burroughs' career into periods of differing interests is contrary to the facts and to the spirit of his life. His earliest writings, like his latest and all in between, show Burroughs to be simultaneously concerned with science, literature, philosophy, and outdoor nature, with only slight changes in emphases at different times.

The student of American literature will inevitably be interested by the part that Burroughs played in promoting and establishing the reputation of his close friend of thirty years, Walt Whitman. To this relationship, so rewarding to both men, I have devoted an entire and rather lengthy chapter. Though Clara Barrus in *Whitman and Burroughs Comrades* has provided a detailed and accurate history of the friendship, no one has adequately gauged its effects on either writer. My chapter on the subject is, therefore, an effort to fill this gap. In addition, Burroughs' early, lifelong, and single-minded recognition of the greatness of Whitman is indicative of the former's true significance in the history of American thought and letters. Though he was at times an original thinker, Burroughs was primarily an interpreter of the American environment to Americans—not only the natural environment but the intellectual, spiritual, and esthetic milieu of which Whitman was an important, though largely ignored, manifestation.

Burroughs both followed and formed the trends of his times. Whitman, Charles Darwin, Henri Bergson, Ralph Waldo Emerson, a score of others, pointed the way; and Burroughs, who was among the first to take the direction indicated, soon found himself at or near the head of an ever lengthening column of like-thinking fellow countrymen. He was never intellectually static but was always adjusting his point of view to new modes of thought and to new discoveries in science. Thus, starting as an Emersonian, he ended his life occupying intellectual positions shared, in part, at least, by men like Wallace Stevens, Theodore Dreiser, and Robinson Jeffers; but he had arrived on the ground long before they did—indeed, had led the way to it. Nonetheless, he never rejected Emerson completely.

Burroughs was outstandingly a harmonizer of seemingly discordant trends in American thought and points of view. He discarded nothing outright, not even Calvinism in its entirety. Consequently, he was able to accommodate Whitman to Emersonian Transcendentalism and Darwin and geology to both. An ardent student of the sciences, with faith in their liberating function in human life and thought, he nevertheless remained always a believer in the ultimate supremacy of spirit over matter. In his intellectual development occurred a pure example of Hegelian synthesis—a union of the opposites of scientific materialism and philosophic idealism. The result was an outlook, widespread among thinking Americans in this century, composed of deistic, humanistic, and unitarian elements, with an infusion of nature mysticism of the Thoreau variety to provide a distinctive American flavor.

An energetic correspondent during all his adult years, Burroughs wrote thousands of letters, many of which still exist. A large number have been published, but a larger quantity may be examined only in libraries from coast to coast. For making these letters and other manuscript material available to me in the original or in Xeroxed form, I am indebted to the staffs of the libraries that are listed on the acknowledgment page that follows this preface. Everywhere—and I attempted to examine all the important collections—I met with the utmost courtesy and consideration. Thanks to this cooperation, I think I have had access to an even greater mass of material than did Clara Barrus, who wrote the definitive biography of John Burroughs. In addition, the interlibrary loan staff at my own State University of New York at Albany worked tirelessly in making available copies of rare editions and other printed materials; my gratitude to them is great.

For information about Burroughs and the town of his birth I owe much to Mrs. Louisa Smith, Secretary of the Roxbury, New York, Burroughs Club. I wish also to record my appreciation for aid and insights given me by Dr. Dean Amadon and Miss Farida Wiley— president and treasurer, respectively, of the John Burroughs Memorial Association and both members of the staff of the American Museum of Natural History in New York. Miss Wiley during a long lifetime has contributed selflessly to the activities of the association and is extremely knowledgeable on the subject of Burroughs' life and work. The volume of selections from Burroughs' writings that she has edited, *John Burroughs' America*, is a monument of good critical judgment. Finally I take pleasure in expressing my gratitude for the help and encouragement given me by Mrs. Elizabeth Burroughs Kelley, John Burroughs' granddaughter, who still lives on the Burroughs estate of Riverby, at West Park, New York. On my visits to Riverby and nearby

Slabsides, Burroughs' woodland cabin, Mrs. Kelley, herself the author of two excellent books on Burroughs, has shared with me her detailed knowledge of her grandfather's life and work and has granted me access to her own extensive manuscript holdings. She also read my completed manuscript and offered many valuable suggestions.

PERRY D. WESTBROOK

State University of New York at Albany

Acknowledgments

Mrs. Elizabeth Burroughs Kelley and Mrs. Ursula Burroughs Love have graciously granted me permission to quote from unpublished letters and other manuscript materials written by John Burroughs, as well as from such of his published writing as is still protected by copyright. I wish further to express my gratitude for permissions granted by the Library of Congress to quote from material in the Charles E. Feinberg Collection of Whitman materials; by the Henry E. Huntington Library and Art Gallery to quote from a letter written by Burroughs to Albert B. Paine; by the New York Public Library to use excerpts from John Burroughs' letters to Myron Benton contained in the Henry W. and Albert A. Berg Collection; and by the University of Virginia Library to quote from materials in the John Burroughs Collection in the Clifton Waller Barrett Library.

Contents

Chronology

1837   John Burroughs born on farm at Roxbury, New York, April 3, the seventh of ten children of Chauncey A. Burroughs and Amy Kelly Burroughs.

1844–   Attended district schools.
1854

1854–   Taught in country schools in New York State, New Jersey,
1863   and Illinois; briefly attended Hedding Literary Institute in Ashland, New York, and Cooperstown Seminary, where he first read Emerson.

1856   His first publication, "Vagaries *viz*. Spiritualism" by "Philomath," which appeared in the Bloomville, New York, *Mirror*.

1857   Married Ursula North, a farmer's daughter of Tongore, New York.

1860   Contributed "Fragments from the Table of an Intellectual Epicure" by "All Souls" and other essays to Henry Clapp's New York *Saturday Press*. His Essay "Expression" published in the *Atlantic Monthly*.

1861   Published his first nature pieces, under the general title "From the Back Country," in the New York *Leader*.

1862   Studied medicine for several months with a physician at Tongore, New York. Beginning of forty-year correspondence and friendship with the farmer-writer Myron Benton of Leedsville, New York. Wrote his most famous poem, "Waiting."

1863   First read John Audubon. Moved to Washington, D.C., where he met Walt Whitman and became his lifelong friend and admirer.

1864   Received appointment as a clerk in the Currency Bureau of the Treasury Department. Continued nature study and writing.

1867   His first book, *Notes on Walt Whitman as Poet and Person*, published.

1871   Visited England on a mission for the Treasury Department. Met Thomas Carlyle. Published *Wake-Robin*, his first volume of nature essays. Second and enlarged edition of *Notes on Walt Whitman as Poet and Person.*

1872   Resigned from Treasury Department clerkship.

1873   Received appointment as special bank examiner. Began building his home Riverby on land purchased at West Park on the Hudson.

1874   Moved to Riverby.

1875   *Winter Sunshine* published, containing further nature studies and an account of his European visit, "An October Abroad." Started vineyard and berry farming at Riverby.

1877   *Birds and Poets* published, containing first extensive literary criticism.

1878   Birth of son Julian.

1879   *Locusts and Wild Honey* published.

1881   *Pepacton* published.

1882   Second journey to England.

1884   *Fresh Fields*, mainly about England, published.

1885   Gave up bank examining.

1886   *Signs and Seasons* published.

1889   *Indoor Studies*, a volume of literary criticism, published.

1892   Death of Whitman.

1894   *Riverby*, mainly nature essays, published.

1895   Built Slabsides, a rustic cabin near his home in West Park.

1896   *Whitman: A Study* published.

1899   Summer voyage to Alaska as member of the Edward H. Harriman expedition with John Muir and others.

1900   *The Light of Day*, a treatise on theology, published.

1901   Beginning of acquaintance with psychiatrist Dr. Clara Barrus, who for the rest of his life was his literary secretary, his typist, and his companion.

1902   *Literary Values* and *John James Audubon* published. Visited Jamaica, West Indies.

1903   Nature-faker controversy begun with publication in the March *Atlantic Monthly* of Burroughs' "Real and Sham Natural History." Accompanied Theodore Roosevelt to Yellowstone National Park, the beginning of a close friendship with the president.

1904   *Far and Near*, a volume mainly of travel pieces, published.
1905   *Ways of Nature* published. Spent part of winter in Bermuda.
1906   *Bird and Bough*, Burroughs' only book of verse, published.
1907   *Camping and Tramping with Roosevelt* published.
1908   *Leaf and Tendril* published. Established as summer retreat Woodchuck Lodge on the home farm at Roxbury.
1909   Journeyed with John Muir in Arizona and California and visited Hawaii.
1910   Awarded degree of Doctor of Letters by Yale University.
1911   Again visited California. Received degree of Doctor of Humane Letters from Colgate University. First read Henri Bergson.
1912   *Time and Change*, on science and philosophy, published.
1913   *The Summit of the Years*, again on science and philosophy, published. Received gift of a car from Henry Ford, whose friend he became.
1915   *The Breath of Life*, a volume focusing on the phenomenon of life, published. Awarded the degree of Doctor of Letters by the University of Georgia.
1916   *Under the Apple-Trees*, musings on life and the universe, published. Awarded Gold Medal for his writings by American Institute of Arts and Letters.
1917   Death of his wife, Ursula North Burroughs.
1919   *Field and Study*, essays on nature and philosophy, published. Winter in California.
1920   *Accepting the Universe*, mainly a scientific and philosophical volume, published. Again wintered in California.
1921   Died March 29, on railroad train in Ohio while returning to New York State. (Two volumes, *Under the Maples and The Last Harvest*, almost completed before his death, were edited and published this year and the next, respectively, by Clara Barrus, now his literary executor.)

CHAPTER I

John Burroughs—A Catskill Farmboy

I   *"Homesickness which home cannot cure"*

JOHN BURROUGHS was born in 1837 on an isolated dairy farm in the township of Roxbury, New York. Situated three or four miles from the village, the Burroughs property consisted of over three hundred acres of upland meadow, pasture, and woods. No lovelier hill country can be found in the eastern United States. Still untouched by tourism or industry, this region of steeply tilted fields is laced by stone walls and winding roads and is watered by clear springs and brooks. The forests along the mountain ridges are mainly composed of hardwood trees that blaze into red and yellow in October and that clothe the slopes in shining green in spring and summer. Especially abundant is the sugar maple, whose flowing sap signals the end of winter and which formerly provided the farmers with as much syrup and sugar as they had the energy to make.

This region is old country geologically and historically. The Catskills are among the most ancient mountains in the world, as their blunted summits testify. The first settlers, Burroughs' great-grandparents among them, came to this area from New England and Long Island during the American Revolution. The soil was good—the deposit of ages of erosion of the mountain ranges by rain and glacial ice—but the fields were littered with boulders and, in exposed places, ribbed with outcropping ledges. As in New England, crops could not flourish until the stones had been cleared from the fields and built into fences. The labor was backbreaking, but these Yankee and down-state farmers were used to it, and they soon made the land blossom with a fertility that remains to the present day. The Roxbury countryside and the Old Home, as Burroughs always called it, held him with an unbreakable attachment and lay, as a primal impulse, at the heart of most of his literary output. One cannot read much of Burroughs' work without becoming intimately acquainted with the area, not only its physical features and natural history, but the spirit of its peaceful beauty.

Burroughs left Roxbury when he was seventeen, never to return permanently. But all his life, even though most of it he lived only fifty miles across the mountains at the Hudson River hamlet of West Park, he was continuously subject to pangs of homesickness—in his words a "homesickness which home cannot cure."[1] Wherever he was—from as far away as Washington, D.C., where he lived for nine years—Burroughs frequently returned to Roxbury, to again share in the life of the farm, in tapping the maples, pitching hay, and cleaning the pasture spring. After his father's death, one or another of his brothers took over the place, and Burroughs still returned for visits. For him it was essential that the farm remain in the family, and when necessary he supplied financial backing to that end. Its loss would have been the loss of a part of himself—that part which was the very foundation of his spiritual and creative life. But retaining the farm was a lifelong struggle and, at times, a harsh one. Only in his last years, after 1913, could he feel secure about it, for at that time his friend Henry Ford bought it and gave it to him outright. Burroughs' attachment to the place strengthened, rather than weakened, as he grew older, and after 1910 he spent long summers in an old house, which he named Woodchuck Lodge, on the east end of the property.

In *My Boyhood*, which also contains reminiscences by his son Julian, John Burroughs gives an impassioned account of his growing up on his father's farm. The facts that he imparts are doubtlessly accurate enough—indeed, most of them can be found here and there in his other writings—but the lyricism of this haunting piece of prose is its important aspect. Written in his seventy-sixth year, it is a sustained paean to his lost youth, an evocation of the scenes and activities of a way of rural life which became extinct long before Burroughs' death, and he never became reconciled to its loss. A truly spiritual autobiography, it explores the sources of its author's strength as a person and as a creator.

One such source, of course, was the natural beauty of his environment and the exposure it afforded him to the ways of birds and wild animals and to the cycle of the seasons. But more basic and more subtle as an influence was the family life in which he had participated on this isolated mountain farm. Both of Burroughs' parents were descended from vigorous yeoman stock. He himself was born the seventh of ten children—six boys and four girls. Neither of his parents nor any of his brothers and sisters was educated beyond the barest fundamentals. Aside from the Bible, a hymn book, a newspaper, and a religious magazine, the household was devoid of reading matter. When John Burroughs became a famous author, none of the family read his books. For long periods his oldest brother, Hiram, a beekeeper who had failed as a dairy farmer, lived with him at Slabsides at West Park. Yet one day when he handed Hiram one of his newly published books with the remark that he had written it, Hiram only stared at its cover and laid it down without a word.

Yet the solidarity, the sense of unity, in such a farm family with its unremitting rounds of toil and chores remained with him. None of the family had either any real sympathy or understanding of Burroughs' way of life, but they loved him and relied on him and thought of him always as one of theirs. Nor did he ever feel separated from them. The death of each parent and each brother and sister—he was the last to die—was a new shock, undiminished by any that had gone before. He mourned each one with equal pangs of grief, and he visited the family graves yearly.

This feeling of oneness with a family among whom he was intellectually an alien is one of the most remarkable, and likable, facets of Burroughs' life. It was an emotional attachment that overrode any other influence or force. Yet it was inevitable. To understand it, one must call to mind the conditions on an early nineteenth-century farm in the back country. The family was virtually a self-sustaining unit; the home acres and animals supplied the food, clothing, shelter, and fuel by which a family survived. The little cash that was needed was gained by the sale of surplus produce—in the case of the Burroughs farm, butter, which the father occasionally carried by wagon to the town of Catskill forty miles away. There were neighbors, of course, most of them quite far off, who would from time to time band together in cooperative projects such as maintaining a district school, repairing roads, or erecting a barn; and in the distant village were artisans, such as blacksmiths and wheelwrights, for specialized services.

But for the most part, a farm family lived by its own labors and resources, each member doing his share indoors or out to wrest a livelihood from the rocky soil. Fortunately the labor, though hard, was varied and called for many skills, so that the routine was bearable and at times fun, as during maple-sugar time. But whatever a family got for itself, whether material or spiritual, it got from hard work done together. To wrench oneself from such a unit, as Burroughs did in his late teens, is to create in one's life a vacuum hard to fill. Burroughs never did fill it. The Roxbury meadows, hills, and pastures exerted their pull on him more because they were associated with the vanished family life that had cradled him into manhood than because of their pastoral loveliness. Hence a return to the home farm, especially in later years, could never assuage his longings. What he needed was a return to his lost boyhood.

Religious observances were not overwhelmingly important in the Burroughs household. The father, indeed, seems to have been the only one with strong religious feelings; and he was a passive man, not one to insist on equal zeal from his family. He belonged to the Old School Baptists—a primitive Calvinist sect which emphasized predestination, election, and conversion by irresistible grace. To these believers, one was predestined to salvation or damnation by divine fiat, and the efforts of the individual or even of the church had little influence in bringing about the conversion that was a sure sign that one was elected to eternal life. Thus, the father felt that, if the children were elected for conversion, nothing he could do would either hurry or delay it; God's inscrutable plans from the beginning of time were all that mattered.

John Burroughs, in fact, did experience during his adolescence a keen interest in religion and perhaps thought he was on the verge of the all-important conversion. But nothing came of it, and the rest of his life he was highly critical of orthodoxy of any sort. Yet he envied his father the comfort of an unwavering faith. At no time did Burroughs sneer at any creed that brings satisfaction to its followers and encourages an acceptable moral code. In himself, moreover, he always recognized a lingering and ineradicable attraction to the basic Calvinist doctrine of predestination. All his life John Burroughs was a reluctant determinist.

II   *John Burroughs and Jay Gould*

In this spiritual and physical environment John Burroughs grew up to become—whether deservedly or not—one of the most influential writers of his times—a man to whom President Theodore Roosevelt addressed the words: "It is a good thing for our people that you have lived. . . ."[2] As shall be seen, Burroughs' influence undoubtedly was benign in many ways; and it would be tempting to credit his rural upbringing with his later very worthwhile accomplishments. Yet there is good evidence that his early life on the Catskill farm was not the sole cause of his later development. It is a curious fact about Burroughs that he actually seemed fated to know and consort with celebrities—such men as Walt Whitman, Theodore Roosevelt, Thomas Edison, Henry Ford.

The first person of fame, or infamy, in his acquaintanceship was Jay Gould, the famous railroad magnate who was born on a farm near the Burroughses and was John's schoolmate and playmate. Burroughs frequently reminisced about this other notable man of Roxbury, and the reminiscences were not flattering to Gould, who at an early age manifested the aggressive, acquisitive traits of character that made him one of the most obnoxious of the buccaneers of finance. These two are the totally discordant products of the same soil and social order. That the peaceful Roxbury hills, the closely knit, cooperative family life of the pre—Civil War northern countryside could nurture such disparate individuals is a problem for sociologists to resolve.

Theodore Dreiser early in his career—even before writing *Sister Carrie*—pondered this problem after an interview with John Burroughs at Slabsides in 1898. In an article based on an interview for the magazine *New Voice*,[3] Dreiser takes as his theme the contrast between the lives of these two Catskill farmboys. Dreiser was at the time interested in such questions as, What makes men successful? What is the definition of success? Many articles that he wrote during the last years of the century explored possible answers. Burroughs and Gould represented to Dreiser dramatically different types of success—that of the quiet artist-thinker and that of the ruthless hoarder of money and power. During the interview, he kept Burroughs on the subject of his relationship with Gould and was rewarded with the anecdote of a wrestling match between the two boys.

Before the match, certain rules had been agreed upon, but Gould, when he found he was losing, broke the rules and won. When Burroughs reproached him, Gould simply answered, "I threw you, didn't I?"[4] The incident, Dreiser and Burroughs tacitly agreed, was an allegory of conscientious passivity vanquished by conscienceless aggression. But Burroughs, who had always considered himself to be a passive observer of life rather than a conqueror, was also an indubitable success and one that Dreiser would temperamentally be drawn to and admire. The spectacle of the philosopher-naturalist in his forest cabin impressed Dreiser deeply, if one may judge from the enthusiastic tone of the *New Voice* article. Yet we know that Dreiser was also fascinated by magnates of business like Gould, who appear in his novels, and who are often set in opposition to artists or thinkers. Indeed, the opposition occurs in his first novel, *Sister Carrie*, which was begun in the same year in which the interview with Burroughs occurred. Carrie initially succumbs to the aggressiveness of the successful businessman Hurstwood;

but, when he is unmistakably headed toward failure, she is drawn to the esthetic and philosophical Jefferson Ames.

One need not suppose that the visit to Burroughs at Slabsides had any direct influence either on *Sister Carrie* or on Dreiser's writing in general. Still, Dreiser must have been acquainted with Burroughs' writing; no person who read the better periodicals of the day could have been otherwise. Burroughs had long been turning his attention to exactly the subjects that were to preoccupy Dreiser most of his life: man's place in nature, evolution, the freedom of the will. Dreiser, the student of nature who later toyed with the religious philosophies of John Woolman and the *Bhagavad-Gita*, had much in common with the naturalist Burroughs, who was so ardent a disciple of Whitman and Emerson. In each, scientific naturalism was tempered and at times supplanted by mysticism.

III   *Departure from the Old Home*

John Burroughs' formal education was sporadic. As a child he attended one-room schools in his district. When he had exhausted their highly limited resources, he did several months of schoolteaching at Tongore in nearby Ulster County, and he thereby saved enough money to support himself for three months at Hedding Literary Institute, actually a high school, at Ashland, New York. Here he took the usual academic subjects and became acquainted with at least the names of the standard English authors, as a list of "Books I *Will* Read"[5] compiled at this time reveals. After another stint of teaching at Tongore, where he fell in love with Ursula North, whom he was later to marry, John Burroughs attended Cooperstown Seminary for the spring term of 1856. He had already become interested in writing, modeling his style on that of his then favorite author, Samuel Johnson—and in the spring of that same year his first effort had appeared in print: an article in the Bloomville, New York, *Mirror* entitled "Vagaries *viz.* Spiritualism," signed "Philomath." In it, he attacked the credibility of mediums, who, he asserted, are afraid to operate "in the *light of day*" but conceal their activities "under the cover of night."[6] The exposing of what he considered a sham was characteristic of Burroughs throughout his life, but the bombastic style of this piece and its cold, fact-bound scientism were not.

At Cooperstown he was beginning to shake the Johnsonian influence, so disastrous to his prose, and was coming under the aegis of Emerson, whose thought became a lifelong guide and whose style became his new model. "It was at this time that I took my first bite into Emerson," Burroughs recalled long afterward, "and it was like tasting a green apple—not that he was unripe, but I wasn't ripe for him. But a year later I tasted him again ... and took a bigger bite; then soon I devoured everything of his I could find."[7] He elsewhere comments: "I read him in a sort of ecstasy. I got him in my blood and he colored my whole intellectual outlook . . . His boldness and unconventionality took a deep hold upon me."[8] And again, he writes, "For a time I lived and moved and had my intellectual being in him."[9] Though the ecstacy passed—Burroughs later realized that Emerson's appeal is strongest to the young—this conversionlike experience changed his outlook permanently. All his life he wrote about Emerson, and one of the last essays from his pen was a lengthy and sensitive appreciation of Emerson's *Journals*. Burroughs was a late but extremely vocal Transcendentalist.

After one term at Cooperstown Seminary, where Burroughs was active in debating and oratory, he taught in schools in New Jersey, New York, and Illinois; but his own formal education was finished. The next year he married Ursula North, the daughter of a prosperous farmer. Like most young men about to be married, he had forebodings about the wisdom of this drastic step; and in some ways the future justified his fears. Ursula was in most respects the opposite of Burroughs; for, as Clara Barrus writes in her *Life and Letters*, "Nature evidently sought to preserve [a] balance by uniting John Burroughs in marriage to a woman who had preeminently certain traits in which he was deficient, notably pride, self-confidence, and aggressiveness" (I, 45). Burroughs was, as has been noted, a passive person, and his passivity was bolstered by his Transcendentalism. His famous poem "Waiting," written a few years later, perfectly records his attitude: one need only wait and one's "own will come" to him.

Burroughs was by nature and conviction, then, a dreamer, a bystander; but Mrs. Burroughs believed in battling life, or at least in having her husband battle it. She considered his writing to be unremunerative dawdling. His satisfaction with its meager returns, added to his income from bank-examining and what he earned from his few acres of vineyard and berry patch, angered her. She seems to have disliked country living, and she spent her winters in Poughkeepsie to avoid the rigors of the snowy months at Riverby. An obsessive house cleaner, who could not tolerate a speck of dust on her floors or a thread of cobweb on her ceilings and walls, she was constantly incensed by her spouse's acceptance of a certain amount of disorder. Needing a "girl" to help with the housekeeping, she was never able to find one who could stand more than a few weeks of her nagging, so that there was a chronic servant problem. Burroughs found refuge in two outlying retreats: first in his Bark Study, so called because of its chestnut-bark siding, and then at Slabsides, his hut in a wooded gorge a mile away. A friendly man, he often wished to bring visitors to his home for an hour's chat or a week's stay, but Ursula usually so resented these intrusions, which to her meant only more tracked-in dirt and additional time over the kitchen stove, that he came more and more to do his entertaining in the privacy of Slabsides, which he built in 1895.

Burroughs often compared himself with his father—a quiet, reserved man convinced that his life was being directed according to God's foreordained plan. Uncomplainingly he had submitted to the ceaseless round of seasonal duties: plowing, sowing, cultivating, haying, harvesting, thrashing, woodcutting, maple-sugaring, and then back again through the same cycle, which of course was superimposed on the daily routines of milking, feeding the stock, cleaning stables, and sawing and splitting stove wood. To the son, the most symbolic of the father's activities was his yearly stint of laying up stone fences—miles of them during his lifetime. The massive walls, most of them still standing, represented to Burroughs something more than mere patience and endurance. They revealed, rather, a faith in a code of living and in one's mission on earth. Persons like his father, John Burroughs thought, must never have questioned the rightness, for them at least, of their farmer's lot. If they were Calvinist, as was Chauncey Burroughs, they then of course knew that their labors were fulfilling God's inexorable will. John Burroughs had from young manhood a similar faith in the rightness of his own literary calling. A written work, he has said, consists of laying words together as a wall-builder fits boulders into his wall. It would take more than an unsympathic wife to deter him from his writing.

During the year before his marriage, Burroughs had decided that he was going to be a writer. He had already had two articles in print—the one on spiritualism, and another on "Revolution," privately printed, which had been issued by a friend in Illinois. More importantly, he had discovered and been fascinated by literature. He had already read much of Samuel Johnson, Alexander Pope, James Thomson, John Milton, and Shakespeare—the standard authors in the schools of his day—and had later experienced in the essays of Emerson a revelation as to the depths and heights of thought and feeling that literature could command.

Some of the old Puritan notion about God's part in selecting one's calling must have lingered in him—a notion fortified by the message of self-reliance at the heart of Emerson's thinking. At any rate, even before his marriage his mind was made up. In a letter to Ursula a week after the wedding, he wrote:

I sometimes think that I will not make the kind of husband that will always suit you. If I live, I shall be an author. My life will be one of study. It may be a weakness in me to cherish the thoughts I do, but I can't help it. I know not why I should not try to realize my aspirations; why I should not strive to rise to that sphere toward which my soul continually aspires. I know I must struggle hard to realize my end, to have my name recorded with the great and good. But if God spares my life, the great world shall know that I am in it. The good, the beautiful, and the true my soul worships; and the more your spirit assimilates to mine in this respect, Ursula, the more I can love you.[10]

IV   *The* Saturday Press

Burroughs was practical enough to know that for a time he would have to earn most of his living by means other than his pen. Yet from now on writing remained the passion of his life. While on one teaching job, in New Jersey, he began writing for the New York *Saturday Press*, an exciting new and, as it proved, short-lived weekly edited by Henry Clapp and including among its contributors many of the bohemian group associated with Pfaff's Restaurant. T. B. Aldrich, Fitz-James O'Brien, Ada Clair ("the Queen of the Bohemians"), and, most important, Walt Whitman, whose "Out of the Cradle Endlessly Rocking" first appeared in the *Saturday Press*, all helped to give the paper a sort of *avant-garde* reputation as well as literary excellence. Burroughs' offerings were a poem, "To E. M. A.," dedicated to his friend E. M. Allen, with whom he shared an interest in writing, and a series of eight prose pieces on a wide variety of subjects, appearing between May 5 and November 3, 1860. Of these, five were collections of paragraphs under the title "Fragments from the Table of an Intellectual Epicure" by "All Souls," a choice of names that Burroughs later regretted. The other three were essays signed with Burroughs' real name: "Deep," "A Thought on Culture," and "Poetry."

If nothing else, the *Saturday Press* contributions prove how profoundly Burroughs had been touched by Emerson. In "A Thought on Culture," he flatly states: "Emerson is the most mature mind in this country; his culture is the most perfect and complete, and to wish him more logical is to wish him to stoop from his high altitude and become less intellectual."[11] Stylistically, the debt to Emerson will become obvious as we examine some excerpts indicative of Burroughs' immersion in Transcendentalism. Most impressive to him was Emerson's thesis, developed at length in *Nature* (1836), that physical nature is a metaphor of God or of the underlying and basic spirituality of the universe. Next to Emerson's influence we see in these early pieces that of Carlyle, whose *Sartor Resartus* would, of course, supplement the ideas in Emerson's *Nature*.

"Deep," Burroughs' first work to appear in a periodical of any reputation, makes the point that mere difficulty of style is not a mark of profundity. On the contrary, the deepest thoughts should be clothed in clear and unpretentious language. In a later *Saturday Press* essay (May 26, 1860) Burroughs singles out Dr. Johnson's prose, which a few years before he had admired, as the opposite of an effective style. Johnson's periods, he quips, act "like a lever to the third kind; the power applied always exceeds the weight raised . . ."(1). To this conviction that simple style is the best Burroughs remained true throughout his life, and to it may be attributed the success of much of his own writing.

He makes in "Deep" (*Saturday Press*, May 5, 1860) a second point that is purely Transcendentalist in its import: "The visible is everywhere the articulated invisible, the finite is the articulated infinite. . . . Every man is part of the Infinite Spirit of the universe, a part of God, but just the moment he becomes man, just the moment he emerges from all Being into any particular type of being . . . he ceases to be Infinite and becomes finite" (2). Thus, a writer, as a finite being addressing himself to other finite beings, must communicate in terms of the finite, that is, by objects, things, which in turn represent the infinite. In this respect the German philosophers fail as writers, for they attempt "to explain thought by thought" (2), not by metaphor, whereas Emerson and Carlyle, with their marked concreteness of diction, brilliantly succeed. "A book must suggest as well as define" (2). The Germans concentrated too much on defining and too little on suggesting, which can best be achieved by metaphor, simile, and analogy. As Burroughs says in his "Fragments . . ." of May 26, "a book that addresses itself at once to the imagination and the common sense, like a day that kisses the branches and penetrates to the roots of a tree, is the best" (1). Or, as stated in the "Fragments . . ." of June 9, "the highest problem of Literature and Art is to lift us up in sight of

... huge possibilities; not to realize and hem us in, but to break down our limitations and let us flow out into open space. Art must not be a wall against which our thoughts rebound, and which narrows and pinches the mind. It must relieve and make the breath come easier" (3).

The same principle applies to education as to writing. In his June 30 "Fragments . . ." Burroughs contends, "We confine the attention of . . . youth too much to Dollars and Cents, and to the Multiplication Table. We had better teach him how to BE than how to know. He is not only to do sums . . . but he is to work out the problem of his destiny on this world's blackboard with the white chalk of truth in his hand, and the love of the Great Master in his heart" (1). For "the uncompromising line of Right belts the world everywhere the same, and the final result of our lives must be measured from it" (1). Another point of reference for such measurement is great men, whose relationship to the commonalty of man is similar to that of mountains to the plains—again a notion obviously derived from Emerson and Carlyle.

In these *Saturday Press* pieces Burroughs was definitely placing himself on the side of spirit, favoring mysticism as opposed to empirical science; but during his lifetime he was to vacillate frequently between the two. Not that at any time he rejected science, but he never was its single-minded devotee. Indeed from this conflict in his spiritual and intellectual life is derived his significance and fascination for his times, for he was experiencing what every other thinking man was experiencing.

V *"Expression" and "Analogy"*

The year 1860 was an extremely successful one for Burroughs as a beginning writer. Not only did he place material with the *Saturday Press*, but he also achieved the ultimate accolade of publishing an essay, "Expression," in the November *Atlantic Monthly*. Written concurrently with the *Saturday Press* pieces, which in places it paraphrases or repeats verbatim, this essay is in a way an orderly summary of his hitherto somewhat haphazardly presented thought. So like Emerson in style and subject matter is it that the editor, James Russell Lowell, checked through Emerson's writings to rule out plagiarism. Since *Atlantic* articles were not signed at that time, others who read Burroughs' essay made the same error. "Expression" is still listed in Poole's *Index* as being by Emerson. Elsewhere it has been mistaken for the work of David Wasson, a frequent contributor to the *Atlantic*.

Nonetheless, in the purity of its Transcendentalism, this essay, no matter how derivative, is a tour de force; it is more than imitation, for it is a deeply felt statement of faith and as such ultimately stems more from its author's inviolable individual personality than from the man who originally sparked this belief within him. Burroughs writes as one who is composing his credo:

Absolute life we can have no conception of; the absolute must come down and incarnate itself in the conditioned, and cease to be absolute, before it comes within the plane of our knowledge. The unconscious is not knowable; as soon as it is thought, it becomes conscious.

And this is God's art of expression. We can behold nothing pure; and all that we see is compounded and mixed. Nature stands related to us at a certain angle, and a little remove either way—back toward its grosser side, or up toward its ideal tendency—would place it beyond our ken. (572)

Through analogy, man perceives hints of the absolute behind the particular and the general: "Analogy is the highest form of expression, the poetry of speech . . . the marrying of opposite facts, the perception of the same law breaking out in a thousand different forms—the completing of the circle when only a segment is given. . . . Without Analogy, without this marrying of the inward and the outward, there can be no speech, no expression. . . . The highest utterance is a perpetual marrying of thought with things" (374-75). Because of the function of material objects as symbols of the infinite, the literary style which most vividly conveys the impressions of things is the most effective. In English, the Anglo-Saxon words do this best and cannot be ignored by a writer. Latin words, which Burroughs defines as the fatty element in the language, are to be employed with restraint and caution.

So excited had Burroughs become about the idea of analogy as the key to understanding the universe, as well as to creating vitally meaningful literature, that he planned to write a book on the subject. The plan never came to fruition, but shortly after "Expression" he submitted to the *Atlantic* the essay "Analogy," which Lowell rejected, doubtlessly because of the resemblance of its content to the earlier essay. But the *Knickerbocker Magazine*, which did accept it, published it as the lead article in its December, 1862, issue. Most interesting in it is a passage emphasizing the relation of the familiar objects of outdoor nature to literature (echoings of Emerson's "The American Scholar"): "We would do well to read in the woods and in the fields: to muse in the barn and in the barn-yard; to court familiarity with cows and sheep, and swine, and hens, and hay-mows; with backwoodsmen, with sailors, with soldiers, with mechanics, with farmers; with all the thousand-fold forms of nature and life, that we may infuse something fresh and real into our culture and speech" (483). Of course, Burroughs followed this suggestion all his life: he went to the fields and woods for the materials, for the words, of his writing—not merely to gather facts for more or less reportorial nature articles. Analogy continued to be a favorite subject of his. In September, 1891, the *Atlantic* took an essay on the subject, which was reprinted in *Literary Values* in 1901.

Before publishing his 1860 essay on analogy, Burroughs had sent it to David Wasson, whose own essays in the *Atlantic* he had greatly admired. Wasson was gracious and frank. He liked the piece, but he warned Burroughs against trying too much in the way of philosophical writing until he was older; and he definitely advised him against the proposed book. He found Burroughs' style satisfactory but a little heavy at times; he predicted improvement with practice. Wasson himself was a farmer's son from Maine, who had had to struggle to break into the world of letters. Perhaps he saw something of himself in this other farmer's son; at any rate, he was encouraging and flattering. Curiously anticipating Theodore Roosevelt's words fifty years later, Wasson wrote enthusiastically: "I augur good for my country from the discovery of every such intelligence as yours, and I pledge to you my warm interest and regard."[12] Burroughs later ceased to admire Wasson, but the boost he had received from him was valuable at the time. With so little formal schooling. Burroughs was in need of any teacher and adviser he could get. Wasson briefly and intelligently served that purpose at a critical time in Burroughs' literary development.

The *Saturday Press* pieces and the essays in the *Atlantic* and the *Knickerbocker* reflected a short-lived but promising phase in Burroughs' career as an author. But he was troubled, and rightly, about his heavy leaning on Emerson in style and thought; and he had the good sense to know that such imitation—even if largely unconscious—had no future. As an antidote, he launched into a series of short essays on farm life for the New York *Leader*, to which he had already contributed several philosophical pieces. These essays "From the Back Country," as he called them, are his initial efforts in the genre of the nature essay that was to bring him his first and perhaps most lasting fame. Written while he was away from home, they are infused with the nostalgia that tinged with melancholy so much of his nature writing all his life.

VI   *Friendships*

While he was teaching in New Jersey, John Burroughs had established a close friendship with a young man from Newark, E. M. Allen, to whom he dedicated his first published poem. More important, Allen shared Burroughs' early interest in Walt Whitman and later, in Washington, D.C., introduced him to the poet. Allen visited Burroughs at the Roxbury farm and camped with him in the Catskills and Adirondacks, and the correspondence between the two was copious and at times ardent. Allen, who was enthusiastic about Burroughs' writing, predicted for him a name to be mentioned with Emerson's and Hawthorne's. Having moved to Washington himself, he urged Burroughs to follow—as he eventually did. For Burroughs, with his limited background, the association with, and the encouragement of, a man of Allen's considerable sophistication and intellectual attainments were important, though it was short-lived. In 1865, Allen married Elizabeth Akers, a poet noted mainly for her lines, "Backward, turn backward, O Time, in your flight,/ Make me a child again just for tonight." Soon the couple moved to Richmond, and the friendship became dormant.

Another friendship was of greater significance because it lasted much longer on an active basis. In early August, 1862, Burroughs received a letter from Myron Benton of Amenia, New York, in praise of his recent articles in the New York *Leader*. One of these essays, "Ways of Power," Benton thought was "full of deep and excellent thought";[13] and he found the sketches "From the Back Country," which had been appearing in the same periodical, charming. He identified himself as a farmer with literary tastes similar to Burroughs'. To this genial letter Burroughs quickly responded, speaking of his own literary interests and activities. The correspondence continued till 1900, during which time Burroughs wrote over a hundred and fifty letters. Soon the two met, and from then on went on camping trips together and visited at each other's homes.

Benton, who idolized Thoreau and had received the last letter ever written by him, was a Transcendentalist in his outlook. First an active and successful farmer, he found time to write poetry, articles, and reviews, all of respectable quality, for current periodicals. Unlike Burroughs, he did not feel that authorship was his destiny, to which all other activities were subsidiary. Burroughs raised grapes and berries in the summer so that he could support his family and still have most of his winters for writing. Benton, as a dairy farmer, enjoyed no such periods of comparative leisure, for cows must be milked and fed and tended the year round. But both were lovers of the land, and Benton's farm, which had the most beautiful spring of water Burroughs had ever seen, rivaled the old farm in Roxbury in the loveliness of its natural setting in the Weebetuck Valley.

The correspondence between these two is fascinating, for it shows the growth and interests of two highly sensitive minds that were dependent on sources other than formal education for their intellectual stimulus. Actually, they stimulated each other by discussions, candid and frank, of books, of fellow authors, and of their own work in progress. They were avid readers of the magazines—the *Galaxy*, the *Saturday Press*, the *Commonwealth*, and above all the *Atlantic*—and would send each other copies of interesting numbers. In letters and in conversations they discussed the authors of the day, such as Carlyle, William Dean Howells, Robert Browning, Henry James, and Whitman, whose *Leaves of Grass* they read together while strolling in the woods of Troutbeck, as Benton called his farm. They read each other's works on occasion and reviewed them in periodicals, and the criticism was always honest and hence constructive.

In difficult times in their personal lives, they would consult together, as during Benton's courtship and Burroughs' period of indecision as to whether he should enlist in the Union Army—which he refrained from doing, partly on Benton's advice. With their philosophic idealism and their passionate love of nature, these two followers of Emerson and Thoreau formed an outpost of Concord in eastern New York—a two-man group which at times was augmented to three by Brownlee Brown, an eccentric truck farmer and Transcendental poet living in Newburgh. Nothing attests more forcefully to the vitality of the Concord way of thought than the stimulus it was to persons like these three countrymen, transforming into adventures of the mind lives that might otherwise not have risen above the routine of farm chores.

CHAPTER 2

Burroughs and Walt Whitman

IN *The Last Harvest*, published posthumously in 1922, Burroughs wrote: "I have always patted myself on the back for seeing the greatness of Whitman from the first day that I read a line of his. I was bewildered and disturbed by some things, but I saw enough to satisfy me of his greatness" (254). He first read some of Whitman's poems as early as 1859 or 1860 in the *Saturday Press*. Among these were "Out of the Cradle Endlessly Rocking" (then entitled "A Child's Reminiscence") and "There Was a Child Went Forth" (then entitled "The Child That Went Forth"). In addition, both E. M. Allen and Myron Benton were admirers of Whitman, and they must have encouraged Burroughs' interest until it became almost an obsession. During the Civil War, Allen had gone to Washington and had there become a good friend of Whitman, whom he had known at Pfaff's Cellar. In his letters to Burroughs, he wrote glowingly of the poet, with whom he had established "the bond of beer."[1]

Finally, half with the purpose of getting into closer contact with the war and half with that of meeting Whitman, Burroughs went to Washington in 1863. Allen, who took him in tow, aided him in finding temporary work in the Quartermaster General's Department. Later he was employed on a more permanent basis in the Currency Bureau of the Treasury Department, where he served as guardian of a vault containing millions in bank notes. Day after day he sat at a desk in front of a steel wall; there was ample time to write, and he made good use of it.

I *Meeting with Whitman*

Shortly after Burroughs' arrival in Washington occurred the event that made the whole venture worthwhile: Allen introduced him to Whitman. Soon the two were fast friends, and they remained so until Whitman's death. By December 19, 1863, Burroughs was writing to Benton: "I have been much with Walt, have even slept with him. I love him very much. The more I see and talk with him, the greater he becomes to me. He is as vast as the earth, and as loving and as noble."[2] Burroughs accompanied Whitman on some of his hospital visits, and Whitman tramped with Burroughs in the nearby countryside. Whitman, who had heard much about Burroughs from Allen, seems to have been pleased with the new friendship, which was to prove a profitable one for him. As time went on and as Burroughs became a nationally esteemed figure with access to all the best magazines, his influence was incalculable in establishing the controversial poet's reputation. Whitman may have had more fiery supporters—for example, William O'Connor— but it is doubtful that he ever had one more effective and persistent. Before his own death Burroughs had published dozens of articles and many lengthy championing letters to newspapers, as well as two books, to present the case for Whitman to the reluctant American reading public.

The two men were certainly what Whitman would call "comrades." In Washington, after Ursula arrived, Whitman frequently dined and breakfasted with the Burroughses. He became attached to Ursula, who was friendlier to him than to most of her husband's literary acquaintances. Later, when Burroughs moved to West Park on the Hudson River, Whitman visited there three times, apparently with great enjoyment if one can judge from his descriptions of the visits in *Specimen Days*. After leaving Washington, Burroughs frequently visited his friend at Camden; and he occasionally spent a holiday with him on the New Jersey coast.

II *The Hermit Thrush*

A lover and close observer of nature, Whitman in the Washington years, and later, found much to interest him in Burroughs' growing expertise on birds. An early and happy result was the introduction of the hermit thrush and its song into "When Lilacs Last in the Dooryard Bloom'd" as one of the major symbols of that poem and as the occasion for the finest lyric passage Whitman ever wrote. In a letter to Myron Benton on September 15, 1865, Burroughs writes: "He [Whitman] is deeply interested in what I tell him of the Hermit Thrush [*sic*], and says he has used largely the information I have given him in one of his principal poems."[3] It is interesting that in the *Atlantic Monthly* for May, 1865, when Whitman must have been working on his great elegy, there appeared Burroughs' essay "In the Hemlocks" (later printed in *Wake-Robin*), in which is a detailed and impressive description of the song of the hermit thrush—the "divine contralto" (*Wake-Robin*, 60), as Burroughs calls it. Doubtless much of what Burroughs told Whitman corresponded to what appears in the essay, which indeed Whitman may have read either in print or in manuscript.

At any rate, some of Burroughs' language is remarkably suggestive of the spirit of what we find in Whitman's poem. To begin with, Burroughs writes that to him the thrush's song reflects "spiritual serenity" (46), which is precisely what is conveyed in the poem. Burroughs is writing about what he has seen and heard at the old farm; consequently, his own description is heightened by a lyricism which momentarily assuages his perennial homesickness:

a strain has reached my ears from out the depths of the forest that to me is the finest sound in nature,—the song of the hermit thrush. I often hear him thus a long way off, sometimes over a quarter of a mile away, when only the stronger and more perfect parts of his music reach me; and through the general chorus of wrens and warblers I detect this sound rising pure and serene, as if a spirit from some remote height were slowly chanting a divine accompaniment. This song appeals to the sentiment of the beautiful in me, and suggests a serene religious beatitude as no other sound in nature does. It is perhaps more of an evening than a morning hymn, though I hear it at all hours of the day. It is very simple, and I can hardly tell the secret of its charm. "O spheral, spheral!" he seems to say; "O holy, holy! O clear away, clear away! O clear up, clear up!" interspersed with the finest trills and the most delicate preludes. It . . . seems to be the voice of that calm, sweet solemnity one attains to in his best moments. It realizes a peace and a deep, solemn joy that only the finest souls may know. A few nights ago I ascended a mountain to see the world by moonlight, and when near the summit the hermit commenced his evening hymn a few rods from me. Listening to this strain on the lone mountain with the full moon just rounded from the horizon, the pomp of your cities and the pride of your civilization seemed trivial and cheap. (51-52)

The similarity between Whitman's and Burroughs' thrushes is evident. The idea of the song's providing spiritual solace, serenity (Whitman uses the word "serenely" in Section 16 of "When Lilacs Last . . ."); its rising above all earthly cares; its fundamental joyousness; the bird's solitary haunts and its predilection for night singing—all are impressions and details shared by both authors. The references to the cities at the end of Burroughs' description and of Whitman's thrush's song seem more than coincidence, and the presence of the moon in

Burroughs' piece parallels that of the evening star in Whitman's, though we know that Whitman had actually observed this preternaturally bright star during the March prior to Lincoln's death.

Burroughs has been praised by bird lovers for his skill in rendering birdsongs in verbal paraphrase. His "O spheral, spheral . . ." in the passage just quoted would appear to be one of his most successful efforts in rhythmic and onomatopoetical reproduction. Yet, while rhythms can be caught quite successfully in such exercises, the actual notes are more elusive. Vowels are all that are useful, since birds do not utilize consonants distinctly; and all the vowels can do is to indicate variations in pitch and in length or quantity. Thus in his reproduction of the thrush's song, Burroughs begins with a long *o*, followed by long *e*'s and *a*'s indicating a rising and falling pitch which persists throughout. To the careful reader, some of this alternation between higher and lower vowel sounds can be detected in Whitman's "carol of death."

As for the rhythms suggested by Burroughs, they are discernible also in the poem, especially in the repetition of certain words and in parallelisms. The first stanza provides typical instances:

> Come, lovely and soothing Death,
> Undulate round the world, serenely arriving, arriving,
> In the day, in the night, to all, to each,
> Sooner or later, delicate death.

Such comparisons are perhaps tenuous, but the fact is that Whitman's elegiac lyric does in sound and rhythm *suggest*, without attempting to reproduce, the hauntingly beautiful song of the hermit thrush as described by John Burroughs and as very likely heard by Walt Whitman in his youth. Whitman, of course, long before he knew Burroughs had been sensitive to the music of birdsongs, as is amply indicated in "Out of the Cradle Endlessly Rocking" published in 1859. Yet Whitman gave credit to Burroughs not only for the idea of using the thrush but also for information about its habits and the quality of its song.

III   *Walt Whitman and His "Drum-Taps"*

In a letter to Myron Benton, written on January 17, 1866, Burroughs inquired: "Have you read *Drum Taps*? There are no other poems in the language that go into me like some of those. I have some immortal times with Walt." On March 20, he wrote again to Benton that the editors of the *Atlantic* had expressed an interest in an article on Walt Whitman so long as it was reasonably objective. Burroughs, thus encouraged, submitted a piece on *Drum-Taps*; but it was turned down by W. D. Howells—in irritation, Burroughs called him "Willie Dear"—who had recently joined the staff. This essay, Burroughs went on to explain, was to be one of a series which was to constitute a book on Whitman. Eventually, *Galaxy* took the essay rejected by the *Atlantic*, and it was published in December, 1866, under the title "Walt Whitman and His 'Drum Taps.' " It was the most perceptive and sensitive criticism of Whitman to appear up to that time, and it may still be read with profit by Whitman students.

The first five pages of the essay are devoted to a sketch of Whitman's life and personality, an account of his work in the Washington hospitals, and some comments on *Leaves of Grass*. According to Gay Wilson Allen, this essay contained the first reliable factual information on Whitman to be published.[4] Moving on to a critique, Burroughs points out the contrast of "the sadness and solemnity of 'Drum Taps' . . . with the flushed, exultant, arrogant, fore-noon spirit of 'Leaves of Grass' " (610). *Drum-Taps,* he continues, is definitely not a book about battles and heroic exploits but one about death and suffering as experienced by the individual soldier mustered from private life in country or in city. For to Whitman, Burroughs informs us, war appeared as only a passing phase in an era in which peace and peaceful pursuits were the norm. Artisans and farmers fought the Civil War, not a warrior class devoted to war as the most noble purpose of existence as in feudal times and earlier. Yet these artisans and farmers in accepting the temporary challenge evinced the truest heroism—that of freemen rather than that of slaves.

But, according to Burroughs, not even the heroism of the common man is the deepest subject of *Drum-Taps*. Basically, the poems are a celebration of death as one of the aspects of nature; and this celebration reaches its climax in "When Lilacs Last in the Dooryard Bloom'd," Burroughs' analysis of which remains valid down to the present day. Pointing out the three primary symbols—the hermit thrush, the evening star, and the lilac sprigs—Burroughs shows how the poem presents, elaborates on, and intertwines these three symbols in the manner of a musical composition, never mentioning Lincoln explicitly but re-creating the sorrow that his death aroused among his countrymen and extending this sorrow to include all the dead of the war—indeed, all the dead of all time. Finally, Burroughs recognizes that the poem is fundamentally dramatic—a presentation of the conflict within the elegist, and by extension within all his readers, between grief for the dead and acceptance of death as part of nature.

IV   Notes on Walt Whitman as Poet and Person

In Burroughs' letter to Myron Benton of March 20 in which he spoke of the *Drum-Taps* article, he outlined the larger study that he planned to write on Whitman. With considerable modification of his original plan, he wrote, revised, and enlarged the book all through 1866, apparently with frequent consultation with William O'Connor and with Whitman himself, whose actual contribution will be considered later. In February, 1867, Burroughs had the book set in type at his own expense; and it was published in June by the American News Company in New York.

When Burroughs first mentioned his project to Benton, he had written that his "drift or conclusion [was] to be that Walt Whitman is a return to Nature—that 'Leaves of Grass' is an utterance from Nature, and opposite to modern literature, which is an utterance from Art; that W. W. gives the analogies of the earth, and that he is the only modern or democratic man who has yet spoken, and our only hope from utter literary inanition."[5] To this thesis the book adheres, as does almost everything else that Burroughs wrote about Whitman. In his first pages and elsewhere, he gives an account of his friendship with the poet. He devotes much space and care to describing Whitman's personality and appearance, for he believed that an idea of these is essential to an understanding of the poetry.

Burroughs makes much of Whitman's manly bearing, and he quotes Lincoln's comment on seeing the bearded poet in the street: "Well, *he* looks like a MAN."[6] This emphasis on physical appearance must have pleased Whitman—he may have suggested it himself—for it was one of his major tenets that a robust body is a prerequisite for a robust spirit, and he always took pains to impress the public with his own health and vitality. But more important, as Burroughs fully recognizes, was what might today be called Whitman's charisma, which Burroughs described as a "magnetism . . . incredible and exhaustless" (13). Whitman's whole person, both physical and spiritual, exerted an irresistible attraction, inspired immediate confidence and good feeling, and gave the impression of an all-embracing compassion and power of love.

Burroughs was fortunate in first becoming acquainted with Whitman

during the Civil War when the poet's personality had reached full
fruition. Whitman himself and most of his critics have realized that the
war years—the years of his total dedication to the care of the wounded
and dying in the Washington hospitals—were the most decisive in his
spiritual and artistic development. There is no understanding of
Whitman as poet or person without full knowledge of this period of his
life, any more than one can understand Dostoevski without reference to
his years in a Siberian prison. What resulted in each case was an
immensely deepened comprehension of what it is to be a human
being—a revelation of the depths and heights attainable by man's spirit.
Burroughs aptly remarks of Whitman's war years, "His whole character
culminates here" (95); and, in the latter part of the volume, he presents
Drum-Taps as the artistic expression of this culmination.

Most of Burroughs' book is a discussion of the entire *Leaves of
Grass*, as it appeared in the edition of 1867. At the start, he takes a
defensive position, one for which T. W. Higginson later chided him.[7]
Against what he thought was the public assumption that Whitman was a
mere pupil of Emerson, Burroughs assures the reader—very likely again
on Whitman's prompting—that, before the 1855 edition of *Leaves of
Grass*, the poet had never read a page of Emerson—an assertion
definitely contrary to facts as one knows them today. In regard to the
widespread accusation that Whitman was an obscene poet, Burroughs
has much to say and says it forcefully. There is animality in *Leaves of
Grass*, he concedes, especially in the long "Walt Whitman" ("Song of
Myself" in later editions); but there is also "aspiration" and even
"mysticism" (26). Whitman insists on accepting man as an entirety
made up of spirit, as well as of a body akin to that of animals.
Certainly, Burroughs insists, Whitman is not licentious. He treats "the
sexual acts and feelings . . . mainly with reference to offspring, and the
future perfection of the race, through a superior fatherhood and
motherhood" (28). He sings of men and women with the innocence of
Adam before the Fall. Giving a clue to many later critics, Burroughs
singles out for quotation Whitman's descriptions of himself as a "chanter
of Adamic song/Through the new Garden of the West. . . ."

The purpose of *Leaves of Grass*, Burroughs finds, is no less than to
present the specifications for a new man, whose physical, mental, and
spiritual attributes will be a model for Americans in future ages. This
new man will not be restricted to any one privileged class but will be
found among the masses. This claim for the potential of the average
man is, to Burroughs, among Whitman's most important contributions.

Only by going beyond culture, beyond civilization, into the area of the natural, the wild—the purely biological that underlies societies—could Whitman find the basis for such faith in the average of mankind. For, like Emerson, Whitman (and Burroughs at this time) saw a continuity between the natural and the social orders. The moral law exists in all nature, and man derives from nature his own ethical and spiritual values and norms. The great poet—in this case Whitman—is more sensitive than others to the spiritual kinship of man and nature and brings an awareness of it to his less perceptive fellow mortals. Thus Whitman, like other Romantics, speaks not from his library or study but from the open air. For ultimately "Nature itself is the only perfect poem, and the Kosmos is the only great poet" (40). The human bard can only echo his cosmic master, nature.

Not that *Leaves of Grass* has outdoor nature as its sole subject; its main subject, rather, is preeminently man as he contains nature within himself—man the microcosm and even the creator of nature. Above all, *Leaves of Grass* is not preoccupied with the wild as opposed to the civilized. A student of Emerson, Burroughs saw in Whitman's concept of nature much more than a revival of Wordsworth's reliance on impulses from a vernal wood. As to Whitman's supposed lack of form or art, Burroughs explains it by saying that there is actually no lack; on the contrary, there is a superabundance of art, that of nature herself. Whitman writes in the form of nature; his book, like the creations of all the greatest poets, is a manifestation of nature.

Using one of Whitman's favorite metaphors, Burroughs asserts that "in Nature everything is held in solution; there are no discriminations, or failures, or ends; there is no poetry or philosophy—but there is that which is better, and which feeds the soul, diffusing itself through the mind in calm and equable showers. To give the analogy of this in the least degree was not the success of Wordsworth [one of Burroughs' favorite poets]" (47). But such was the success of Whitman, whose book Burroughs considers to be the most significant literary production of its or any other time.

As for the presence of beauty in *Leaves of Grass*, Burroughs resorts to an image that was to reappear many times in his work—the presentation in mythology of beauty mounted on a lion. Whitman, of course, had refused to exclude evil or ugliness from his vision of the universe. Much energy has been expended by critics in trying to explain Whitman's attitude toward the evil and the ugly, of which he insisted he was the poet as much as of the good and the beautiful. Burroughs' explanation is more convincing than most: to him, the ugliness in the world is the lion upon which beauty rides; similarly, one presumes, evil would be the lion upon which goodness rides. According to the Emersonian law of opposites, there can be no beauty without ugliness. Along with the loveliness of nature are the coarseness, the crudity, the cruelty everywhere apparent in her. Homer found beauty in war; Dante, in hell; Whitman, in the midst of chaos and darkness. Or rather beauty emerges, without being actually sought, from the poet's rendering of nature in all her facets, both the appalling and the inspiriting ones, all of which are integral to the universal scheme.

Burroughs, as has been observed, rightly singled out as Whitman's major purpose in *Leaves of Grass* the sketching of a new man, a New World personality to tally with the promise of America. Since, as Whitman and Burroughs saw it, the American idea is based on the potential growth of the individual, the function of the poet in releasing and guiding this potential, once it is set in motion, is indispensable. Yet all the poet can do is to present himself as the liberated individual that all can potentially be. In terms of myth, the new American is the new Adam ready for a fresh start in a new Eden. Whitman's poetry is a prophecy of the new order, and Whitman himself served in the same way as an Old Testament prophet instructing the chosen people in the ways of the Lord.

But prophecy may be condemnatory, foreboding, as well as exhortatory. *Leaves of Grass*, Burroughs maintains, stands as a crashing rejection of everything in American life that is shoddy, flabby, corrupt, or grovelingly imitative of Europe. So far, the Garden has produced mainly weeds with a few stunted specimens of human flowering. American poets ignore the one basic truth about man: that he "is the crowning product of God, of Nature, because in him all that preceded, and all that exists in objective Nature is resumed. ... He is a living proof that every single atom of dust is capable of vital life and divine inspiration. Without him Nature, though living, is dead. He vivifies it, blends it, as the body blends with and becomes dear to the soul. He only, finally, *is* Nature entire" (67-68). A human being is thus to be held in reverential awe. Literature must be measured by its success in conveying that awe, and in this respect *Leaves of Grass* meets every test.

In Burroughs' essay on *Drum-Taps* he had already recognized that Whitman is a supreme poet of death. This point is developed in the second edition of *Notes on Walt Whitman as Poet and Person*, which appeared in 1871; and Burroughs may have used the words of Whitman himself, who, as will be seen, had a hand in the production of both editions of this book. In this same year of 1871, the fifth edition of *Leaves of Grass* had appeared, with the notable addition of a cluster of poems including the great hymn to death, "Passage to India." Burroughs (and probably Whitman) felt that this new *Leaves of Grass* was sufficient occasion for subjoining seventeen pages of supplementary notes to the original *Notes*. The new pages are a conglomeration of information concerning Whitman himself and his critical reception, as well as an explanation of the arrangement of the poems. In this latest form, the conclusion is, *Leaves of Grass* "is an expression, more decidedly than before, of that combination in which Death and the Unknown are as essential and important to the author's plan of a complete human Personality as Life and the Known" (112). For the passage to India is more than a voyage of geographical or even intellectual discovery; it is much more also than a celebration of the achievements of nineteenth-century engineering. It is, above all, a voyage of discovery into the realms of the spirit transcendentally conceived, and especially into that realm where the spirit finds its ultimate fulfillment in the death of the body

Thus, as Burroughs pointed out in *Notes, Leaves of Grass* has undergone in successive editions a steady growth toward what it was all along destined to be and has finally become in 1871 — a poem "of the absoluteness of Spirit" (114). In Whitman's words,

> There is nothing but Immortality,
> The exquisite scheme is all for it;
> And Life and Death are for it.

Paralleling German idealistic philosophy, *Leaves of Grass* becomes the greatest poem of the nineteenth century, which Burroughs considers the most significant century in human history. Like all true interpreters of their times, Whitman also anticipates the future and thus outstrips his contemporaries and receives their jeers for being a visionary, a crackpot, or a liar. These insults the future will disregard.

V *Authorship and Reception of* Notes

There has been much controversy as to how much of *Notes* was actually written by Whitman. Estimates have varied from almost the whole book to only rather small portions. The question is an important one, especially for Whitman scholars, who would like to know whether the book supposedly written by Burroughs should be added to the Whitman canon as a major statement of the purposes of his poetry. The problem has been carefully considered by Clara Barrus in *The Life and Letters of John Burroughs* and *Whitman and Burroughs Comrades*; and the concerned reader would do well to examine her conclusions.

Clara Barrus was prodded into making a full presentation of evidence after a certain F. P. Hier, Jr., had published an article in the *American Mercury* of April, 1924, claiming that Burroughs had admitted to him in a letter that the book was almost entirely Whitman's. What prompted Hier to make what is obviously an irresponsible claim is not clear, especially as he had corresponded with Burroughs under an alias. At any rate, it was the sort of sensationalism and iconoclasm—since it tended to show both Burroughs and Whitman as fakes—that the editors of *American Mercury* enjoyed publishing. Fortunately, Clara Barrus had copies of the letters that Burroughs had sent to Hier, and she had gleaned other information directly from Burroughs, who remembered that Whitman had done considerable editing of the *Notes* and of some later writings. Burroughs frequently submitted his work to his friend for suggestions. Sometimes these suggestions would constitute a sentence or occasionally even a paragraph, which Burroughs would incorporate verbatim into his text. "Whitman's mark," he wrote Hier, "is on several of my books and magazine articles which were written during the Washington days. He was a great critic, and I was in the habit of submitting my Mss. to him for his strictures."[8]

Specifically, according to Burroughs' own account, Whitman renamed the *Notes*, "pruned it, and reshaped many of the paragraphs."[9] He worked over the biographical materials in proof and added or corrected them, but apparently orally; and—though Burroughs was not sure of his memory here—he contributed in their entirety the "Supplementary Notes" to the second edition. Finally, Whitman wrote the approximately six hundred words of Chapter 21. The two parts of the book which Burroughs singles out as being totally untouched by Whitman are the sections on beauty and those on *Drum-Taps*, the latter being taken from the 1866 article that Burroughs had written while Whitman was away on an extended visit to New York. Since the *Drum-Taps* review contains the germs of most of the other ideas developed in the *Notes* and is the best written part of the book, the basic ideas of the larger work would be logically attributable to Burroughs. Indeed, in the letter (March 20, 1866) to Benton in which he tells about writing the piece on *Drum-Taps*, Burroughs includes an outline—somewhat modified later—of the projected work. Nowhere in those letters to Benton in which he mentions his progress on the *Notes* does Burroughs even hint at a collaboration with Whitman. Furthermore, very extensive portions of a first draft in Burroughs' hand exist in his notebooks for that period.

Among Hier's arguments several might be glanced at. Although according to Hier, Whitman had once actually told a friend that he had written the *Notes*, in many other places Whitman referred to it as being the work of Burroughs. The remark reported by Hier could be the result of faulty memory or of approaching senility. More cogently Hier argues that the book is written in a style suggestive of Whitman's prose, a fact that Clara Barrus also noticed. This is in truth the case, but anyone with an ear for style can detect that the sections, such as Chapter 21, admittedly written by Whitman are much more characteristic of him than other sections that Burroughs claims as his own. In vocabulary and complexity of sentence structure the following, from the last paragraph of Chapter 21, is obviously Whitman's: "We have swarms of little poetlings, producing swarms of soft and sickly little rhymelets, on a par with the feeble calibre and vague and puerile inward melancholy, and outward affectation and small talk, of that genteel mob called 'society.' We have, also, more or less of statues and statuettes, and plenty of architecture and upholstery, and filagree work, very pretty and ornamental, and fit for those who are fit for it" (39). But the following (from the next paragraph but one) is in its economy of words, simpler sentence structure, and lower emotional key obviously Burroughs': "He [Whitman] says plainly enough: I do not wish to speak from the atmosphere of books, or art, or the parlor; nor in the interest of the elegant and conventional modes. I pitch my voice in the open air" (39). Here are Whitman's ideas in Burroughs' words.

Most of the book is written in the style of the second excerpt, but there are traces everywhere of the Whitmanesque, especially in vocabulary. All his life Burroughs as a stylist was plagued by a tendency to imitate favorite authors. He was well aware of this and fought it, usually with success, though he never was able permanently to free himself of an Emersonian influence. Seeing Whitman almost daily, reading his writing, and admiring him as highly as he did, there is small wonder that tokens of this familiarity should be apparent in his own prose. Burroughs for over two years had been immersed in Whitman's manner of thought and feeling.

Like O'Connor, who Burroughs in a letter to Edward Dowden much later says also helped him with *Notes*, he had come deeply under the master's influence, and similar thoughts sometimes tended to find expression in similar language. While he was writing the book, Whitman and O'Connor would doubtlessly be on hand for frequent conversations either about its progress or about ideas that would eventually have to find their way onto its pages. In one sense, *Notes* was a collaboration of these three and others; but a similar statement could be made about many books. An author is inevitably influenced by his associates, his reading, his general environment. Burroughs did the bulk of the actual writing, organized and arranged the thoughts, contributed much of his own that was original and profound, included much, consciously and unconsciously, that had emerged from reading and from conversation with Whitman and other friends. It was his book, as much as any book is one man's—perhaps more than most; for it never had the very real benefit of being worked over by a professional editor.

Notes on Walt Whitman as Poet and Person did not enjoy large sales, for its subject was not a popular one at the time. Most of the first edition remained piled in Burroughs' parlor, but a few copies got into the hands of discriminating readers. The first book-length criticism on Whitman, it was competent criticism, though some modern readers might object to its author's expressions of personal enthusiasm. A number of favorable reviews appeared in this country, including one by Myron Benton for the *Radical*. In England, it received praising notices, among others one by William Rossetti in the London *Chronicle*. Doubtlessly *Notes* helped promote the literary reputations of both its author and its subject.

VI   *Genius and Beauty*

During the period between the two editions of *Notes*, Burroughs' enthusiasm for Whitman remained at fever pitch. His letters to Benton are full of tidings of the poet's activities. He praises highly a series of articles that Whitman was doing for *Galaxy* on "Democracy," "Personalism," and "Literature." Burroughs, too, had written an essay, "Before Genius," for *Galaxy* (April, 1868) which, though it alludes only in passing to *Leaves of Grass*, constitutes an encomium and critique of it as a work of art. During the time Burroughs had been working on this article, he wrote to Benton that he had devoted a whole winter—that of 1867-68—to "writing upon the subject of Art—literary art—with a view to settle in my own mind the question as it relates to 'Leaves of Grass.' "[10] One conclusion is "that a work of art differs from a didactic or philosophical treatise in this, that it is not a thought, but an act, as Creation is; it is the deed transferred to a higher plane, and implies a like totality of the human being."[11] A result of his winter's labors was the essay "Before Genius," which is paralleled by passages from his notebooks of this period. One of Burroughs' profoundest statements on the nature of art, it records his own lifelong convictions on the subject.

"Genius and culture," Burroughs finds, "are not enough" (157)[12] for great creativity, because these qualities must rest on a basis far more elemental than intellectual capacity or attainment. Like Sigmund Freud, Burroughs is postulating a biological source of all manifestations of the human mind and personality. The poet must possess the fundamental strengths—a "plentiful supply of arterial blood" (166)— before he can compose great poetry. If a particular society lacks endurance, heroism, or greatness, it can produce skillful literary technicians, perhaps, but not great poets. The artist must carry the highest potentialities of his race within him before he can express them; and, if his race or epoch is lacking in potentialities—that is, has alienated itself from the forces of nature that underlie all life or has slighted these—then the artist cannot achieve creativity of the first rank. In other words, like Adam's naming of God's creatures, the great artist must avail himself of primitive powers and of the primal materials alone or he will be a mere imitator. He must draw only upon the fundamentals, the first and the best, in his own nature: "With him it is always the first day of creation, and he must begin at the stump or nowhere.... Before Genius is manliness" (166-67).

Corollary to the idea that creativity of the first order is an upsurging of a primal biological force is Burroughs' contention, similar to Whitman's, that contemporary literature is superficial, anemic, and dyspeptic. Encrustations of genteelism and materialism have smothered health-giving impulses in modern society, which in turn has produced a race of feeble versifiers, including most of the "classic" ones of New England. Emerson and Carlyle are the only authors of the century, other than Whitman, who are spiritually alive and truly creative. Whitman is the most vital of these because he has most vigorously rejected the shams of the day. Like Dostoevski's "underground man," though constructively rather than destructively, elemental human spirit has emerged in the person of Whitman whose barbaric yawp has proclaimed to his generation what it is to be a man rather than a mannequin or some other artificiality. He reveals to us our true selves.

Burroughs' concept of genius must be considered in relation to his remarks on beauty in *Notes on Walt Whitman as Poet and Person*. When he included "Before Genius" in his book of essays *Birds and Poets* (1877), he placed immediately after it an essay titled "Before Beauty," which is adapted from the *Notes*. Beauty, he contends in both places, also springs from sources underlying all human personality: "before beauty is power" (167). Beauty to Burroughs, as we have already seen, is aptly depicted in myth as riding upon a lion. Beauty is allied with power, or terror, or fate. It is never an end in itself, as the poetasters have tried to make it, but an accompanying result of natural processes with other ends than the production of mere prettiness. Beauty seeks out the great artist; he does not seek it as a separate entity. Works produced by a strong, manly character are inevitably beautiful, as are all results of nature's basic activities.

One cannot consciously fabricate beauty, nor can one stand aloof and look at it. One must participate in it, for the roots of beauty are in the beholder's deepest personality, as they are in the artist's. An objective beauty is an impossibility, a contradiction of terms. To repeat, beauty in both its producer and its beholder arises from forces that are at the foundation of all life—that bring life into being. It has its origins in the life principle itself; it is ultimately biological. Like genius, it stems from libido (a term not known to Burroughs, of course)—and thus this essay, taking its clue from Whitman, anticipates Freud by four decades. Antithetical to art, with its origins in the deepest instinctual, emotional, and biochemical recesses of the mind and body (that is, in the id), is science, which is a function of the conscious intellect alone.

The title *Birds and Poets* derives directly from the train of thought of these two early and germinal essays that are included in it. One of the other essays, the title one, which first appeared in *Scribner's* in 1873 as "Birds of the Poets," does deal with poetic treatments of various birds and does so interestingly and informatively. But it would be unthinking to ascribe the name of the book solely to the presence in it of this essay in which, in fact, Burroughs denies that to a poet of any stature a bird, be it skylark, nightingale, or hermit thrush, is merely an interesting object on which to try his descriptive skill. Rather, the "bird is a symbol and a suggestion to the poet. A bird seems to be at the top of the scale, so vehement and intense is its life—large-brained, large-lunged, hot, ecstatic . . ." (4). The bird, then, is a life symbol. Burroughs is attempting to account for the fact that many of the greatest poems by the greatest poets—Whitman, Shelley, Keats, Words-worth, Shakespeare—are not about birds but are attempts to reproduce the song and what the song suggests. There is no sentimentalizing here; Burroughs is simply stating a fact—that birds have been a major preoccupation with many great poets—and he explains the fact by pointing out that, like the bird's song, great poetry has its origin in the heart of life.

In his ornithological writing Burroughs frequently made the point that the song of the bird is not basically a sex attribute; it is rather a welling forth of the life principle, an expression of an overabundance of life, an exuberance stemming from an instinct for life that is more fundamental even than sex—so fundamental, indeed, that its origin can almost be said to be biochemical. He makes a similar assertion about great poetry: "All the master poets have in their work an interior, chemical, assimilative property, a sort of gastric juice which dissolves thought and form, and holds in vital fusion religions, times, races, and the theory of their own construction, flaming up with electric and defiant power,—power without any admixture of resisting form, as in a living organism" (173).

The poet then senses in the bird's song the overflow of the same life forces that make him a poet. For similar reasons, spring is one of the prototypal themes of poetry, for this season is the time when the life forces—which are the origin of poetry—are most potent, having awakened from the dormancy of winter. In another essay in *Birds and Poets*, "Spring Poems" (which appeared in shorter form as "Spring and the Poets" in *Appleton's Journal*, June 11, 1870), Burroughs admits that April *can* be "the cruelest month" because in it hope sometimes "assumes the attitude of memory and stands with reverted look" (122)—an excellent statement of the theme of T. S. Eliot's *The Waste Land*. But, in general, the reverse is true: hope, life, and creativity rise strongest for the poet, as for all nature, in April.

VII   *Interim*

All four of these last essays were written in their first form during the time of Burroughs' most intense speculation on the greatness, to him, of *Leaves of Grass*. Though all of them, except "Before Beauty" as it appeared in *Notes*, were ostensibly statements of general esthetic theory, they are actually essays about Whitman; and their readers seem to have accepted them as such. The overall effect must have been beneficial in furthering Whitman's cause and in inveigling the public to take him seriously; but they also aroused some antagonistic controversy. Thus T. W. Higginson's "genteel" sensitivities were so irritated by the slighting remarks on culture, especially that of the eastern seaboard, in "Before Genius," that he wrote Burroughs a lengthy letter of polite protest. Burroughs replied by restating and clarifying his views, but Higginson was never convinced and later became an outspoken disparager of Whitman, thus incurring Burroughs' scorn and anger.

After the publication of the essay "The Birds of the Poets" in 1873, Burroughs' preoccupation with Whitman and the problems of his poetry slackened. During these same years he had been writing a series of nature essays, which had been published in the volume *Wake-Robin* in 1871; and he was now devoting more and more time to nature writing. In 1873 he resigned from his job in Washington and established himself as a vineyarder on the Hudson River near Esopus at what is now the village of West Park. He had bought a tract of land on the river's edge in 1873 and had constructed an imposing stone house, later known as Riverby. Being a realist, he knew he could not support himself and his wife solely by his writing and by his grape growing, at least for a time. He thus took the position of national bank examiner for the Hudson Valley and several other districts, work which occupied him somewhat less than half of each year. Consequently, for three or four years Burroughs ceased to write about Whitman, but he by no means lost interest in him or his affairs. To Burroughs the promotion of *Leaves of Grass* and of the reputation of its author in a world hostile to both was a joyously undertaken duty. He was always ready to cross swords with any belittler and to welcome any newcomer into the ranks of sympathizers. Less volatile than O'Connor, he was perhaps more persuasive and certainly no less untiring in his defense of Walt, who recognized in Burroughs one of his most faithful and effective champions.

When Burroughs next wrote about Whitman, he was not in a meditative or a philosophical but an angrily combative mood. The occasion was a letter to the New York *Daily Tribune* (April 13, 1876), which had published an editorial derogatory to Whitman while at the same time praising the standard New England poets. Though Burroughs' letter is highly subjective in places—for example, he states that he has obtained priceless moral and intellectual gifts from Whitman and his work—it is impressive in its mustering of names of eminent foreign critics who had approved of *Leaves of Grass* and in its arraignment of the majority of the respected poets of the time for inane sweetness, elegance, and artificial correctness. He protests that it is a "disloyalty to Nature to say Whitman has no form,"[13] and he closes with an effusion on Whitman's feeble health but ever cheerful disposition. A purely polemical writing, it doubtlessly served to keep Whitman's name before the public.

VIII   *"The Flight of the Eagle"*

Much more substantive—in fact, one of Burroughs' finest essays among the fifty or so of his on Whitman—is "The Flight of the Eagle," which he wrote in late 1876 or early 1877 and included in *Birds and Poets* in the latter year. Burroughs took the manuscript of this essay to Camden for Whitman to read. "We talked about it—what had best go in, and what were best left out, but he was provokingly silent about the merits of the piece."[14] Among what went in were passages composed by Whitman himself, notably the delightful anecdote of his holding a distraught mother's crying child on a streetcar at the same time that he took over the duties of the exhausted conductor, who had left the car to get his supper. The incident is vividly and humorously told, and it is appropriate to the essay in that it demonstrates Whitman's rapport with the common people and their intuitive trust in him.

The leading idea of "The Flight of the Eagle" is that Whitman is a specimen of complete and consummate humanity—a totality. The essay immediately preceding it in *Birds and Poets* was devoted to Emerson, and there was reason for the juxtaposition. For Burroughs' chief point about Emerson was that, despite his great strengths and merits, he was *not* a totality but rather "an essence, a condensation" (180). Burroughs does not share the surprise expressed by many that Emerson, after his first enthusiastic endorsement of *Leaves of Grass*, cooled toward Whitman. To Burroughs, the wonder is that Emerson was ever enthusiastic about the book at all, so different were the two men. Burroughs' point is a shrewd one and should be borne in mind by those who insist that Walt Whitman is basically a disciple of the Concord Transcendentalist. Whitman, by his own admission, owed much to Emerson, as did Burroughs; but both developed in directions not taken by Emerson. For, as Burroughs has pointed out, Emerson's thought through the fifty years of his career is masked by an almost rigid unchangeability. If Emerson appealed to the young, the young often outgrew him; but they did so, ironically, under the master's stimulus.

The title, "The Flight of the Eagle," is borrowed from a comment in a highly laudatory essay on Whitman that appeared in the Danish magazine *For Ide og Virkilghed* (*For the Idea and the Reality*): "there is an electric *living soul* in his poetry. . . . His flight is the flight of the eagle" (208). The reference to the *living* quality of the poet's soul and the comparison to the great bird are of special significance to Burroughs. To him, Whitman was one of the supreme geniuses precisely because of this vitality and power, both of which are typified by birds, especially by the eagle. Burroughs' critique of Whitman in this essay is not only comprehensive but also perceptive to a degree not surpassed by critics down to the present. Indeed, little has been said about Whitman in the twentieth century that Burroughs had not already said in the nineteenth and much of it in "The Flight of the Eagle."

Burroughs follows his usual practice of providing, as a foundation for his remarks, a personality sketch of the Whitman he had known during the Washington days. On the physical side, Burroughs emphasizes Whitman's robust health, his kindly face, his shapely head; on the spiritual, the profound sympathy and understanding of the man as exemplified in his ministrations in the Washington hospitals. Whitman, Burroughs is careful to establish, does not fit the stereotype of the poet or the artist; instead, he resembles an antique hero—"a sweetblooded, receptive, perfectly normal, catholic man, with, further than that, a look about him that is best suggested by the word elemental or cosmical" (211). Throughout the essay Burroughs reverts to Whitman's health and spiritual power, for beyond all modern poets Whitman embodies these necessary prerequisites for great song.

Burroughs confesses that his own grasp of Whitman's poetry is incomplete. Be that as it may, his interpretation is well worth following. The first of his perceptions—one hinted at in the *Notes*—is that *Leaves of Grass* is the drama of Whitman himself, his relation to his times and to the cosmos, and, as such, it is the drastic representation of all mankind in these relationships. Second, Burroughs stresses the completeness of the poet's absorption and assimilation of nature, the term "nature" being used here in the Emersonian sense to include all objects, even artificial ones, that exist outside the self. Thus, sanity is restored by Whitman to one's views of the body and its functions, especially the taboo functions of sex. For Whitman—a third point—recognizes the truth, all but forgotten in his and later times, that identity "comes through the body" (230), and thus the body must be celebrated in poetry and art as coequal with the soul.

A fourth insight has to do with structure and technique. Burroughs believes that *Leaves of Grass* is lacking in form in the conventional sense but that it coheres through being a dramatic presentation of its author's personality. He describes the individual poems as pulse beats from the center of the poet's being, from which they can never be separated. Thus, the numerous lengthy catalogues, which many find objectionable in Whitman's poetry, have a wavelike quality radiating outward perpetually from the poet's being and experience.

As an aspect of Whitman's absorption of all nature, Burroughs is deeply impressed by his assimilation of contemporary science, which either informs or colors most of his major work. Previous poetry, Burroughs finds, has been grounded mainly in myth; Whitman is the first poet to turn decisively from myth to exact science. "*Leaves of Grass* is, perhaps, the first serious and large attempt at an expression in poetry of a knowledge of the earth as one of the orbs, and of man as a microcosm of the whole, and to give to the imagination these new and true fields of wonder and romance" (242). The terror and superstition of older times are at an end, and man is ushered, by Whitman, into a new paradise of knowledge and faith. The idea that the New World may be a second Eden in which a new man is given a new start is, of course, basic to *Leaves of Grass*; but Burroughs seems to be the first to recognize that fact. To this scientific paradise the poet is essential. With a gentle and beneficent nihilism he must eliminate the dead tissues from the living tradition; he must completely grasp the sciences, which will supplant moribund fable, realizing always that there is poetry in geology and astronomy as well as in myth; and he must act as a corrective to that tendency of science to "forget Man" (246). This last function that science had thrust upon poets was of the utmost importance to Burroughs, who all his life was ambivalent about science; he admired its liberating powers but deplored its way of diminishing human stature. The poet, having mastered science, must transfer to it the emotions of reverence, awe, and wonder that formerly were directed toward myth; for, without these qualities, man becomes a mere mechanism. This humanizing function Burroughs thinks Whitman admirably performs.

Another point that Burroughs resolutely insists upon is that Whitman is a mystic—mysticism being defined as "cosmic emotion" (251), a phrase he attributes to Professor W. K. Clifford. Though this emotion reaches peaks only in certain places in *Leaves of Grass*—for example, in the passage beginning "Smile, O voluptuous, cool-breath'd earth!"—Whitman "never fails to ascend into spiritual meanings. Indeed, the spirituality of Walt Whitman is the chief fact after all, and dominates every page he has written" (262).

As a final insight—one still not shared by many readers of Whitman—Burroughs understands that *Leaves of Grass* in its completed form was a product of the Civil War. To Whitman his ministrations in the Washington hospitals, as has already been seen, was a transforming experience. In the Civil War years Whitman's sympathy—his salient quality as man and poet—underwent full and final development; and it infused his book from then on as a divine breath. Rightly Burroughs ends his essay with comments on Whitman's *Memoranda During the War*, the account of his nursing activities, which "reveals the large, tender, sympathetic soul of the poet even more than his elaborate works, *and puts in practical form that unprecedented and fervid comradeship which is his leading element. It is printed almost verbatim, just as the notes were jotted down at the time and on the spot*" (258). The latter part of the quotation was not italicized in Burroughs' essay, but it is here to indicate that it is an addition to the text by Whitman in his own words. He wished to emphasize the importance to him of the war years in the fruition of his personality. Burroughs was ready to comply.

IX   *Whitman at Riverby*

In the same year, on March 21, took place the first of the three visits that Whitman was to make to Riverby in three successive years. Burroughs described the first as "a great event."[15] Of the second two, Whitman wrote accounts for the New York *Tribune*. He later included extracts from these articles in *Specimen Days*, in which the entry for June 21, 1878, gives an engaging indication of the joy both the guest and the host got from these visits. Whitman in this passage also vividly catches the atmosphere of Riverby, an atmosphere that can still be felt on its secluded acres above the busy river:

"Happiness and Raspberries"
Here I am, on the west bank of the Hudson, 80 miles north of New York, near Esopus, at the handsome, roomy, honeysuckle-and-rose-embower'd cottage of John Burroughs. The place, the perfect June days and nights, (leaning towards crisp and cool,) the hospitality of J. and Mrs. B., the air, the fruit, (especially my favorite dish, currants and raspberries, mixed, sugar'd, fresh and ripe from the bushes—I pick 'em myself)—the room I occupy at night, the perfect bed, the window

giving an ample view of the Hudson and the opposite shores, so wonderful toward sunset, and the rolling music of the R.R. trains, far over there—the peaceful rest—the early Venus-heralded dawn—the noiseless splash of sunrise, the light and warmth indescribably glorious, in which, (soon as the sun is well up,) I have a capital rubbing and rasping with the flesh brush—with an extra scour on the back by Al. J., who is here with us—all inspiriting my invalid frame with new life, for the day. Then, after some whiffs of morning air, the delicious coffee of Mrs. B. with the cream, strawberries, and many substantials, for breakfast.

No better description of Riverby has been written, and no one, probably, ever enjoyed a stay there more than Whitman. In the daytime, Burroughs took his guests on walks or lengthy drives along the main roads or to wilder scenes farther back in the hills. On these outings, Whitman seemed exceptionally alert to the sights and sounds around him. The friendship of the two attained its fullest flowering during these visits. After 1879 Whitman, mainly because of failing health, did not return to Riverby; but they frequently wrote to one another, and Burroughs was constantly in correspondence with Whitman's friends at home and in England in efforts to spread the poet's influence and win for him the reputation that was his due.

In the early 1880s Burroughs was in close contact with Dr. Richard Bucke, a Canadian psychiatrist and mystic philosopher, who saw in Whitman an outstanding example of "cosmic consciousness," an advanced stage of human awareness possessed by only a few in the nineteenth century but, according to Bucke, ultimately to be common to all mankind. Bucke had embarked on a biography of Whitman and requested Burroughs' aid, which was joyfully granted. The correspondence between the two continued long after the biography was written and after Whitman's death, for their admiration of the poet was a bond of friendship not to be broken. Later, Burroughs helped Bliss Perry with his biography of Whitman. Indeed, to the present day no student or biographer of Whitman can progress very far without close and careful consideration of Burroughs' knowledge, both factual and intuitive, about him. More than Horace Traubel, who knew Whitman only in his later years, and more than O'Connor, whose quick temper frequently clouded his judgment, Burroughs remains the most reliable recorder and reflector of Whitman's spiritual and literary development from the Civil War until his death in 1892.

X   *Whitmanmania*

Burroughs, in the decade or so before Whitman's death, had come to regard him with something like a religious veneration. "Whitman is the Saviour, the Redeemer of the modern world," Burroughs wrote to Bucke in 1880, "and his gospel cannot have too many and too fervent preachers."[16] This tendency to regard Whitman as something more than human was of long standing. In a notebook entry for August 26, 1865, Burroughs marvels: "What a wonderful man Walt is; what a great, yearning love he has; what a hospitable soul; what soft, gentle ways; what a deep, sympathetic voice!"[17] And a little later he adds: "Notwithstanding the beauty and expressiveness of his eyes, I occasionally see something in them, as he bends them upon me, that almost makes me draw back. I cannot explain it—whether it is more or less than human. It is as if the Earth looked at me—dumb, yearning, relentless, immodest, inhuman. If the impersonal elements and forces were concentrated in an eye, that would be it. It is not piercing, but absorbing and devouring—the pupil expanded, the lid slightly drooping, and the eye set and fixed."[18]

Usually Whitman's eyes or facial expression did not induce in Burroughs this incipient panic or uneasiness, but he was always overwhelmed one way or another. In a journal entry for February 17, 1877, he writes: "It is a feast to me to look at Walt's face — it is incomparably the grandest face I ever saw—such sweetness and harmony, and such strength—strength like the Roman arches. . . . If that is not the face of a poet, then it is a face of a God. None of his pictures do it half justice."[19] Burroughs constantly alluded to Whitman's appearance and physical bearing. In a letter to Bucke in 1881 he deprecates the rakish-looking picture of Whitman with a hat, the photograph that was printed with the first edition of *Leaves of Grass.* Such a portrait is unworthy, he writes to Bucke, of a man whom they both agree is not simply "a poet, a maker of verses . . . [but] a great and astounding religious teacher."[20]

Burroughs in actual fact did regard Whitman as the founder of a new religion. If this qualifies him as one of the "hot little prophets," as Bliss Perry described those whose enthusiasm for Whitman seemed to get out of bounds, so be it. It is, in truth, puzzling that this farmer, this close observer of nature, this part-time bank examiner, should have been so overwhelmed. Yet time and again he gives evidence that he was. In a fragment unpublished during his lifetime—apparently the notes for an address at a meeting honoring the dead Whitman—Burroughs suggests that the gathering be regarded as a religious occasion in which each participant could confess his "experience" (note the theological word) of Whitman's "Grandeur." Whitman alone, Burroughs goes on to say, "redeems and justifies" (the language of Calvinism) America and has proved America to be a second Israel: "The race and land that can produce such a man as Whitman is in favor with the powers that rule this world."[21] This utterance is an extravagance comparable only to Nicholas Berdyaev's claim for Dostoevski, whose greatness he considered such "that to have produced him is by itself sufficient *justification* [italics added] for the existence of the Russian people in the world; and he will bear witness for his countrymen at the last judgment of the nations."[22] Yet Burroughs resolutely opposed, in letters to Bucke after Whitman's death, the founding of a Whitman Society, for it would be a narrowing and excluding force—directly the opposite of the spirit of *Leaves of Grass*, which Burroughs thought was destined to be the bible of the race.

XI   *The Death of Whitman*

The death of Whitman was, of course, a devastating blow to Burroughs, even though it came not in the least suddenly. Before Whitman had actually died, Burroughs had been asked to speak at the funeral, which was expected momentarily. But he declined, not feeling himself suited or strong enough for the task. Several months earlier, at another moment when death seemed imminent, Burroughs had hurried to the poet's bedside. This was the last time the two were together, and Whitman's final words were, "It's all right, John," an utterance which Burroughs thought referred to his friend's approaching death. When the end finally did come on March 26, 1892, Burroughs attended the funeral, at which he was an honorary pallbearer. Only on his return to Riverby did the full force of the blow strike him. In a letter to Dr. Bucke on April 15, 1892, he wrote: "I thought I was prepared for Walt's departure from this world, but I find I was not. He leaves a bigger void than I thought possible."

To his friend Ludella Peck, a professor of elocution at Smith College, Burroughs laments: "I am just back home from the funeral of my great friend, and am a good deal broken up. I . . . am under a strange excitement which I do not clearly comprehend, my heart beats so loud and strong that it disturbs me when I try to sleep."[23] He says that he has written much about Whitman during the past winter—a renewal of an old preoccupation, sparked by the approach of his friend's death, that will continue for five or six more years. At the end of April, he again writes to Miss Peck; but his thoughts are no longer wholly on Whitman but on death as the universal lot of man. He regrets that he lacks Whitman's faith in immortality, though at times he can bring himself almost to share it. But ultimately death to Burroughs seems nothingness: "We are simply sponged off the blackboard of existence, and the great Demonstrator goes in with new figures and new problems."[24]

In his diary Burroughs records his grief without restraint. On April 6, he addresses Whitman as "Dear Master" and tells how he has begun the annual spring cultivation of the soil. As in "When Lilacs Last in the Dooryard Bloom'd," the April aspects of nature best expressed Whitman's grief for the dead president, so to Burroughs the springtime renewal of the earth adds poignancy to his woe. Other diary entries for that spring exhibit an almost pagan distress: "The world so sweet, so benignant these days, yet my thoughts are away in that Camden cemetery where the great one lies." "W. W. is the Christ of the modern world—he alone ... shows it divine; floods and saturates it with human-divine love." "I am fairly well these days but sad, sad. Walt constantly in mind. I think I see more plainly how Jesus came to be deified—his followers loved him; love transforms everything. I must still continue my writing about him till I have fully expressed myself."[25] Burroughs was not one quickly to forget his personal losses. His grief for Whitman was slow in abating. Years afterward the old poignancy would recur, especially in the spring.

Burroughs was accurately self-analytical when he remarked that he was under a necessity to write about Whitman until he had achieved full expression of himself. In 1892 alone, the year of Whitman's death, he wrote eight articles on his dead friend; and in the next four years he published no fewer than seventeen treatments of one sort or another of the poet, among them his second book on him, *Whitman: A Study* (1896). After these works, as if he had finally satisfied a compulsion, his writing on Whitman slackened but by no means ceased. He had now established himself without really trying to do so as a leading expert on the author of *Leaves of Grass*, and he was asked to do the things that are expected of experts. He made speeches on Whitman, he wrote introductions to at least four volumes of Whitman's writings, he wrote the *Encyclopaedia Britannica* articles on Whitman (for the tenth and eleventh editions), he corresponded and consulted with Whitman scholars like Bliss Perry and O. L. Triggs, and he continued to write magazine pieces wholly or in part about Whitman.

Always Burroughs was a champion, always on the lookout for any slight to his beloved friend. One such occasion was provided when the old enemy, T. W. Higginson, in an attack published between Whitman's death and funeral, accused the poet of having brought on his paralysis and continued ill health by his youthful debaucheries. Burroughs responded to this vicious and unfounded accusation with a slashing rejoinder, printed in the *Critic* of April 9, in which he protested that Whitman, far from being a debauchee, had led a clean, wholesome life. Burroughs, probably correctly, attributed the paralysis to the strain of his hospital work during the war. But the need for these defenses was no longer so great as in the past, for Whitman was slowly becoming accepted in America and much more rapidly in England. His friends could devote most of their energies now to the more constructive activity of interpreting his work.

XII   *"Whitman Land"*

Whitman: A Study (1896), which contains the essence of all that Burroughs had thought and written about Whitman up to that time, lacks emotional outbursts but still emphasizes the overwhelming significance of Whitman in humanity's spiritual evolution. Its completion not only marked a diminution in Burroughs' personal grief for his friend but also coincided with a return of general tranquillity to his life—a shift to a more speculative turn of mind that continued until death. The period about to begin resembles what, in the lives of Hindu sages, would be termed the forest years, the years in which the aging man—Burroughs was almost sixty—removes himself from the material concerns of existence and retreats into some sylvan spot for contemplation. In the first chapter, "Preliminary," Burroughs writes that these initial pages are being composed and the whole book is being revised at Slabsides, the cabin he had recently built in a wild ravine among the hills a mile west of Riverby. This remote and rugged area, where he spent a large portion of his remaining days, he had named Whitman Land, because here he seemed best able to attune himself to the spirit of the poet.

For, as has been mentioned, to Burroughs, Whitman was first and last a supreme manifestation of nature; in this fact lay his greatness and his uniqueness. As epigraphs for the book Burroughs quotes from

Hyppelyte Taine to the effect that "all original art is self-regulated"; from John Ruskin, that "good Gothic . . . has the sort of roughness and largeness and nonchalance" that reflect the "broad vision and massy power of men who can see *past* the work they are doing, and betray here and there something like disdain for it"; and finally from Charles Sainte-Beuve, that in the nineteenth century excitation of the reader's imagination rather than adherence to esthetic rules and formulas is the chief intention of great art. The "naturalness" of Whitman, then, lies in his reliance on his own inspiration as an outflowing of the world spirit and on his refusal to channel this current into conventional literary forms. Throughout the book Burroughs places the, to him, tradition-bound Tennyson in contrast with the unfettered Whitman—always, of course, to the advantage of the latter, though Burroughs had some admiration for Tennyson.

After the Preliminary section has introduced the reader to the rugged beauties of Whitman Land, Burroughs provides the lengthy chapter "Biographical and Personal," which adds little to the information contained in the then long-out-of-print *Notes on Walt Whitman as Poet and Person*, from which Burroughs extracts certain portions to use in his new book. The emphasis is on the "democracy" of Whitman, his comradeship with stage drivers and soldiers; his work in the Civil War is again accorded the prominent treatment that it demands. To demonstrate Whitman's spiritualization of his war experiences, Burroughs inserts verbatim many of his comments in the 1867 essay on *Drum-Taps* (used also in *Notes*). He quotes a statement made by Emerson to Moncure Conway about Whitman: "Americans abroad may now come home: unto us a man is born" (57). Burroughs recounts his own close friendship with Whitman in the Washington years from 1863 to 1873 and the continuing frequent visits with him until his death. As usual, much is made of Whitman's appearance, here presented as a combination of robustness and benignity; and Conway is quoted as saying he thought the poet an avatar of Buddha.

Uniquely, Burroughs believes that in Whitman there was a balance between the physical and the spiritual and a subordination of the intellectual to both that was not to be found in any other nineteenth-century man, assuredly not in Emerson or Thoreau. Whitman is the "strong Adamic man,—man acted upon at first hand by the shows and forces of universal nature" (72). But, despite Whitman's balance of body and soul, he was to Burroughs a supreme spiritualist, for whom the soul engrossed and absorbed the material world and for whom the idea of the brotherhood of man was the guiding principle of existence.

The remainder of the book Burroughs devotes to chapters on Whitman's ruling ideas and aims; his self-reliance; and his relation to art, life, culture, and country. Unfortunately, in this latter two-thirds of the volume, Burroughs is annoyingly redundant, a blemish that he himself admitted in a letter to Dr. Bucke. He had already said most of what he had to say—either in this book or in previous writings. Yet the emphases are sound and deserve a brief examination. So far as Whitman's ideas and aims are concerned, little has been added by later critics to Burroughs' analysis, and most have not been generous in assigning credit to Burroughs. No one has better understood Whitman's purpose of blueprinting a new democratic personality for the fulfillment of the ideals of the new American democracy—using his own personality and its unfolding potential as the only model with which, as a poet, he could be adequately acquainted. By his utter candor in revealing himself, including the sensuality he shares with the rest of humanity, Whitman offended the squeamish of his era; and Burroughs did a service in vehemently defending, when such a defense was most needed, Whitman's frankness as necessary in his program of presenting man in his totality of body and soul. This insistence on full self-revelation is an instance of the self-reliance that Emerson had preached and that Whitman practiced.

Also stemming from Whitman's self-trust is his apparent imperviousness to unfriendly criticism, such as that of Algernon Swinburne, who had once been an admirer but later a disparager. Whitman was willing to wait, beyond his death if necessary, for the reading public to catch up with his ideas. Self-pity and complaint about his neglect, Burroughs not altogether correctly thought, were inconsistent with Whitman's character. Convinced that each man contains within himself a spark of divinity, Whitman was satisfied to rely on the authenticity of his own inspiration and on the future greatness of the as yet tradition-bound American reader. Whitman's confidence in his own ability to live up to the divine best of which man is capable made him seem vain to many, just as his habit of standing outside himself and constantly observing the effect he was creating made him at times appear a poseur—which he actually was, but for reasons other than self-conceit. Attempting to make himself the model of the future American, he perforce had to look at himself and the figure he cut. This objective self-examination really constituted a losing of self and an enhancement of spiritual selfhood through giving himself to others.

Burroughs is weakest in his discussion of Whitman's relation to art. Characterizing him as "an immense solvent" and asserting that "forms, theories, rules, criticisms, disappear in . . . his pages" (116), Burroughs largely overlooks Whitman's meticulous revisions and rearrangements of his poems from edition to edition of *Leaves of Grass*. All America, all of nature and life are engulfed in his pages; and Burroughs tacitly would have the reader believe that search for conventional form in these masses of material would be futile and fatuous. Reverting to an underlying thesis of his study—that the chief purpose of art is to produce strong effects—Burroughs finds Whitman measures up completely. Any conscious artistry in the attempt to produce compelling effects would be not only superfluous but probably detrimental. Impulse becomes the key word; Burroughs is eminently the proponent of "literature of power," of which he considers Whitman's work a superlative example. "His book is not a temple: it is a wood, a field, a highway; vista . . ." (136), the last Whitmanesque word being one of Burroughs' favorites in describing the poet's significance. Whitman opens up for the reader vistas of the future greatness of man and of America; he does not lead us along narrow garden paths of Tennysonian prettiness and formalism. Whitman sought to be a great man, a great comrade, rather than a great poet.

Thus, Burroughs observes, Whitman is not a seeker of surface beauty. He takes and conveys beauty as he finds it incidentally to his absorption of the whole of nature. As has been seen, a cardinal belief of Burroughs' is that beauty is found in a context of much that is ugly and evil. In the deserts grow flowers, out of war emerge reconciliation and comradeship—but the desert and the war cannot be ignored. They are as much the artist's concern and material as the good that they appear with. Whitman refused to paint over the blemishes in his vision of the world. "Beauty always follows, never leads the great poet" (156). Like music, Whitman's poetry is suggestive rather than specific. It embodies no apparent program of philosophy or esthetics, but it provides both of these by suggestion for the receptive reader. Above all, Whitman eschews the merely "literary" utterance that is void of passion for nature and life. Always he strives to generate what Burroughs calls the "cosmic emotion"—a sense of the grandeur and unity of all men and things—and his poems, swept along on the wave of this emotion, drive straight to the soul and thus fulfill the function of the highest art.

In Whitman's poetics—or lack of them—he approximates the

absolutely natural. Similar also is the case with his approach to morals, science, religion: he always relies upon nature. Thus the body as a part of nature must be the equal of the soul; and the Edenic innocence regarding the functions of the body, as a part of nature, must be restored if man is to be healthy either physically or spiritually. In one sense all is good—"Whatever is, is right"—since all is part of nature. But Whitman does not deny the existence of evil, as some of his Transcendental contemporaries tended to do. Since everything in nature is not beautiful and since there could be no concept of the beautiful if ugliness did not exist, so goodness could not exist without evil—and, in this sense, evil serves good purposes; evil indeed is not evil. Thus Whitman's poems embrace good and evil, in the same way that the poet, like all individuals, must share in the good and evil of the world and in the merit and guilt of each person in it. There is a community of guilt along with one of goodness, and every person dwells in both. Only those who are aware of their own human stature—their greatness—as sharers in beauty and ugliness, good and evil, the spiritual and the material—are worthy of citizenship in a truly democratic society. "Man is broad, too broad, indeed. I'd have him narrower," says Dostoevski's Dmitri Karamazov. "What to the mind is shameful is beauty and nothing else to the heart. Is there beauty in Sodom? Believe me, that for the immense mass of mankind beauty is to be found in Sodom . . . The awful thing is that beauty is mysterious as well as terrible. God and the devil are fighting there and the battlefield is the heart of man."[26]

Actually, of course, neither Dmitri nor Dostoevski would have man narrower, any more than Whitman would; for what makes man truly godlike is that he can simultaneously carry in his being the "ideal of Sodom" and "the ideal of the Madonna," and neither "ideal" can exist without the other.[27] If the new Democratic man that Whitman is modeling in *Leaves of Grass* is to possess full human stature, he must possess the all-embracing "broadness" of nature, which includes not only the songbird but the snake that devours the bird. Though Burroughs himself does not draw these parallels with Dostoevski, they are helpful in making clear his interpretation of Whitman.

Burroughs also makes the point that Whitman is a law unto himself since, as a part of nature, he abides only by nature's law. Nor does he, any more than nature, attempt to superimpose a system of philosophy on the scheme of things. He presents the reader with the reality but no explanation of the riddle of being: "It is this that distinguishes the artist from the mere thinker or prose-writer. The latter tells us about a thing; the former gives us the thing, or the spirit of the thing itself (203).

The basic impulse in *Leaves of Grass* is comradely love; the poet gives totally of himself, and this giving is fundamental not only to his esthetics but to his ethics. Not a preacher, not a moralist in the conventional sense, he would inspire his fellow men by the Christlike strength of his love for all mankind, including the most sinful. "He brings to bear character rather than precept" (206), and his own life is his poem as well as his sermon. "The apostle of the idea that man is an indivisible fragment of the universal Divinity" (213), he "appears as the Adamic man re-born here in the nineteenth century" (216). In other words, he is—or would be—what he preaches; and hence he need not preach but merely state what he is. "The poet stands in the garden of the world naked and not ashamed. It is a great comfort that he could do it in this age of hectic lust and Swinburnian impotence—that he could do it and not be ridiculous" (222). To Burroughs, Swinburne, indeed, is almost an antichrist, a representative of all that is artificial, shallow, and ineffectual in poetry and life. Whitman is not actually a poet at all in the commonly accepted sense of the word; he is a prophet whose prophecy is his own life and character. His function is to show his fellow mortals what a man is or what a man can be.

Burroughs also shows that Whitman's poems are a sweeping criticism of American culture, not in its potential but as it actually exists, especially in regard to the engrossment of the individual in the meanness of its norms and the massiveness of its materialism. To Whitman's and Burroughs' thinking, Americans have mistaken refinement for culture; and refinement is too often a *con*finement of the human potential, whereas true culture liberates this potential into flourishing growth and expression. Thus, talent is mistaken for genius, and truly great souls—the Whitmans and the Tolstoys—are overlooked in favor of the Swinburnes and the Tennysons, and literature itself comes to be regarded as a mere "luxury" (243) and not as an essential nourishment for the spirit of man. "The decadence of literature sets in when there is more talent than character in current production" (239). Whitman's mission, far from that of being an entertainer, is to show man a way to the acceptance of his lot as a human being in the New World as revealed to him by the sciences—that is, to lead him from his partial humanity of the past to the full humanity of the future. Whitman wishes nothing less than to save modern man, especially American man, for the life of the spirit.

Burroughs concurs with the opinion of Thoreau and others that Whitman is the first and greatest poet of democracy, combining a "sweeping cosmic emotion" (257) with an inclusive rapport with the masses and asserting the immanence of God in man and nature—the first American poet with continental vision. In comparing Whitman to Emerson—"our divine man, the precious quintessence of the New England type" (269)—Burroughs finds the former much more representative of American modernity, which he defines as a combination of humanitarianism and the individualism that Emerson championed at the expense of altruism. "Whitman is a projection into literature of the cosmic sense and conscience of the people, and their participation in forces that are shaping the world in our century" (273). Emerson, on the other hand, is the poet of the private man and hence is in tune with only one of the two major tendencies of the modern spirit. Emerson stops with the individual conscience; Whitman embraces the mass conscience.

In Whitman's relation to science and religion, he is as much a world poet for his era as Dante and Shakespeare were for theirs. Taking in his stride the scientific discoveries of his century, not yet assimilated by most poets, Whitman engrafts them to his world view. To him, science does not diminish man, as narrower minds believed; instead, it enlarges and ennobles his spiritual stature by revealing the unbelievable grandeur of a universe which exists for and in the divinity of the human soul. The older religions—which Whitman discards—were incapable of generating this vision of man's centrality in the universe and thus inevitably clashed with science. But, since science is a reality that must be dealt with, the old religions must give place to a new one—the Transcendental religion of which Whitman's poetry is an ultimate statement: "The earth is as divine as heaven, and there is no God more sacred than yourself. It is as if the world had been anew created, and Adam had once more been placed in the garden—the world, with all consequences of the fall purged from him" (291). The mood of this new religion is, of course, joyous, triumphant, self-confident, as opposed to the cringing fear and self-loathing fostered by the older faiths. Death, rather than being a terrifying prelude to a day of judgment before a wrathful God, becomes an "exquisite transition" (293).

XIII *"The One Mountain in Our Literary Landscape"*

At the end of *Whitman: A Study* Burroughs protests: "I have accepted Whitman entire and without reservation. I could not do otherwise. . . . I look upon Whitman as the one mountain thus far in our literary landscape. To me he changes the whole aspect, almost the very climate, of our literature" (297-300). One is reminded of Shatov's protestations in Dostoevski's *The Possessed*: "I believe . . . I believe . . . I believe."[28] Like most mortals, Burroughs needed something, and some one, to believe in; and Whitman filled this need. Yet, in Burroughs' later years particularly, he was not totally uncritical in his acceptance. As has been remarked, he could not share Whitman's faith in immortality. As, in his last twenty years of life, Burroughs became more and more preoccupied with science, philosophy, and theology, he explored intellectual seas uncharted by Whitman. His discovery of Henri Bergson's creative evolution is a case in point. Though there is nothing in Bergson's thought to prove Whitman basically wrong, there are areas where considerable mental agility is needed to bring the two together. But this squaring of Whitman with each new development in his own thinking was a necessary activity with Burroughs, and he usually succeeded. It is rare to find a serious philosophical essay from Burroughs' pen in which Whitman is not at least mentioned; and of course these allusions in books and in articles, published in the most respected magazines and by a man whose name was now a household word among all Americans who engaged in serious reading, added impetus to the growing reputation of the poet, who was soon to be a contender for the position of America's greatest.

To see how Burroughs to the end of his life continued to cling to Whitman in his own thinking and to promote him before the public, one may examine the references to him in *Accepting the Universe* (1920), the last of Burroughs' books to be published before his death. By this time, he had become extremely repetitious in what he wrote about Whitman, but this fact in itself is significant in demonstrating the depth of his devotion. In the first essay in the volume, "Shall We Accept the Universe," Burroughs perforce grapples with the problem of the coexistence of good and evil and follows the familiar Whitman lead in not denying the existence of both. The reasoning is essentially that developed over fifty years earlier in *Notes on Walt Whitman as Poet and Person* and again in *Whitman: A Study*. In another essay in *Accepting the Universe*, "Natural Providence," Burroughs reduces his own religious feeling to the thought expressed in one short verse from *Leaves of Grass*: "I have positively appeared. That is enough" (110).[29]

Fittingly Burroughs' last essay, "The Poet of the Cosmos," in this last volume published during his lifetime, is devoted exclusively to

Whitman. In language already familiar, but somehow not stale, Burroughs designates Whitman "as the greatest personality—not the greatest intellect, but the most symbolical man, the greatest incarnation of mind, heart, and soul, fused and fired by the poetic spirit—that has appeared in the world during the Christian era" (316). Burroughs concedes that *Leaves of Grass* is not poetry in the most commonly accepted sense of the word. It is much more than all but the greatest poetry, for it is a reviver of the spirit and a renewer of faith. An understanding of Whitman is aided little by other books but is greatly enhanced by a firsthand knowledge of nature. He grants further that Whitman celebrates and shares in the sin of mankind and the universe. As poet of the cosmos, he could do no less; for sin and evil are part of the cosmos. To the complaint that Whitman considers evil to be "just as perfect as good" (320), Burroughs answers that the adjective is *perfect*, not *desirable*. But, beyond all other considerations, Burroughs, like Thoreau and Dr. Bucke and so many others who knew Whitman, lets the poet's greatness rest upon "his humanity, his primitive sympathy, the depth and intensity of his new democratic character" (322).

CHAPTER 3

Criticism of Emerson, Carlyle, and Thoreau; Esthetics

I   *"The greatest and most typical of all New-Englanders"*

IN 1882 Burroughs wrote in his journal: "Emerson was my spiritual father in the strictest sense. It seems as if I owe nearly all, or whatever I am, to him. I caught the contagion of writing and of authorship before I knew his books, but I fell in with him just in time. His words were like the sunlight to my pale and tender genius which had fed on Johnson and Addison and poor Whipple. . . . I must devote the day to meditating on Emerson, the greatest and most typical of all New-Englanders."[1]

In the long run, it is a question whether Emerson or Whitman had the greater part in shaping Burroughs' attitudes and thinking. So far as genre and prose style are concerned, Emerson, of course, was by far the more powerful influence. Whitman was primarily a poet; and Burroughs, like Emerson in the bulk of his output, was an essayist. Once or twice Burroughs attempted to write verse in the Whitman manner, but with disastrous results. His forte was prose, and in that Emerson was his mentor. From the point of view of literary and intellectual history, then, the Burroughs-Emerson relationship is significant in that it constitutes a remarkable instance of the durability of the Transcendental way of thinking and of the continuing presence of Emerson as a force in the life of the mind in America.

For Burroughs' prestige from 1880 or 1890 until a decade or so after his death must not be underestimated. It is not an exaggeration to say that he enjoyed an esteem and respect comparable to Emerson's. Thus, if he was importantly instrumental in establishing Whitman's reputation, he was similarly so in perpetuating Emerson's reputation and in reinterpreting his views in the light of more recent science.

With Emerson, Burroughs was not emotionally involved in a friendship as he was with Whitman. He had, in fact, no more than a passing personal acquaintance with him. In 1863, while teaching at Highland Falls, Burroughs had met Emerson after a lecture the Concordian was giving at nearby West Point. The meeting was valuable mainly as a thrill, as were the later occasional meetings between the two. Despite the honor of having published his "Expression" in the *Atlantic Monthly*, Burroughs was not happy about the essay's being mistaken for Emerson's, as no Emersonian could be and still follow the doctrines of "Self-Reliance." In the nature, or "Back-Country," essays that he turned to in an effort to find his own style, Burroughs was reasonably successful in shaking off the influence of his mentor. Yet his writing throughout his life met the requirement of Emerson's tenet that in good writing "words become one with things." And always Burroughs remained a strongly metaphorical writer, following the contention of Emerson's essay "Nature" that the material objects of nature are metaphors of spiritual realities.

Thus, while Burroughs was generally successful in forming his own distinctive style, his convictions as to what constituted effective prose were so similar to Emerson's that he occasionally resembled him rather closely. The following passage from *Winter Sunshine* (1875), still an early work, is an example of what could occur in any of his books, but more frequently near the beginning and end of his career. To mistake it for Emerson's would not disgrace the most acute literary critic: "Who ever breasted a snowstorm without being excited and exhilarated, as if this meteor had come charged with latent aurorae of the North, as doubtless it has? It is like being pelted with sparks from a battery. . . . When I come in at night after an all-day tramp I am charged like a Leyden jar; my hair crackles and snaps beneath the comb like a cat's back, and a strange, new glow diffuses itself through my system" (8-9).

In 1877 Burroughs wrote his first ambitious essay on Emerson, included in *Birds and Poets* that same year. In it he presents, in germ at least, most of what he was later to say on the subject. He begins with an acknowledgment of his own great personal debt, for Emerson's raising of the intuitions above the intellect had awakened Burroughs as a youth as it had so many other youths of his generation. Among those who write from the heart rather than from the head, Burroughs ranks Emerson near the top. In this estimate of the appeal of Emerson to the young, Burroughs is in agreement with James Russell Lowell, whose famous essay on "Emerson the Lecturer" records the same charismatic effects. Emerson's writings and lectures functioned with Burroughs exactly as, according to "The American Scholar," literature should: it provided a stimulus, a catalyst, but not a rigidly formulated doctrine as to how the scholar or writer should think, act, and create.

But even in this early essay, Burroughs includes reservations as well as praise. He finds in Emerson an illustration of both the losses and the gains undergone by the race on its transplantation from Europe. The gain is in the direction of clearness, elevation, purity, and boldness of thought, all of which qualities Emerson superlatively exemplifies. On the other hand, he exemplifies the losses, which are failures in the sheer vitality and the power necessary to the highest order of genius. Because of this lack, Emerson falls short of supreme greatness.

Specifically, Burroughs finds Emerson to be too much the New Englander. Since New England has a great deal to offer, Burroughs does not consider that he is insulting Emerson; the point is that Emerson presents in an excessively pure distillation New England qualities at the expense of the most fundamental human qualities. Employing a medical vocabulary which he had learned during a brief spell of apprenticeship to a physician in his youth, Burroughs describes Emerson as "undoubtedly deficient in viscera, in moral and intellectual stomach, but . . . of a fibre and quality hard to match in any age or land" (179). The descendant of an ancient line of preachers and teachers, he conveys in his works the quintessence of the Puritan scholarly tradition and spirit; but, as a result, he is lacking in the coarser, more robust qualities that make for the greatest artistic achievement. His spirit transcends the body to the extent of excluding body. His utterance runs to moralizing rather than creativity. Lacking the earthy qualities, he lacks also the sympathy, the compassion for humanity, that would round out his genius. A coolness, an aloofness, even an intellectual snobbery tend to dehumanize his pages.

Nevertheless, Burroughs thinks Emerson's works are slated for immortality. Despite his deficiencies, which make him less than such prototypal, visceral geniuses as Homer and Shakespeare—despite, to put it bluntly, Emerson's lack of guts—he did, nevertheless, write from his intuitions as well as from his intellect, and herein lies his salvation. Because of his elevation of the intuitions above the intellect (the reason above the understanding, in the language of Transcendentalism), he commands the perennial attention, Burroughs feels, of youth and genius; thus, he will live. To Burroughs, for all his devotion to science, the heart is ever more important than the head.

One of the points for which Burroughs admires Emerson is his ability in his literary works "to clothe science with flesh and blood, to breathe into it the breath of life . . ." (*Indoor Studies*, 77), as he says in a later essay, "Science and the Poets," first published in 1888. This contemporaneity of Emerson's and the receptivity of his mind to the new combine with his essential spirituality to make him an author whom one can reread—whom one can turn to again and again and find refreshing and inspiring. For the man of genius may "no longer [be] at ease in Zion" (*Literary Values*, 133); he must write for his times and from some relevant philosophical basis. Emerson is archetypal in uniting the role of the preacher with that of the imaginative writer. He never ceased being a preacher, Burroughs thinks, despite his withdrawal from the organized church.

Burroughs' writings on Emerson, produced over a period of sixty-two years, would fill a thick volume. Since much of this writing deals with Emerson's thought, it will be considered in a later chapter; but a sizable portion of it, like that which we have just been examining, assesses and describes Emerson's purely literary qualities. Of course, Burroughs' admiration did have its ups and downs. For instance, there were times when he was quite disappointed, if not angry, with Emerson for not continuing to champion later editions of *Leaves of Grass* as he had the first. He was especially piqued when Whitman was omitted altogether from *Parnassus*, an anthology of poetry that Emerson edited. But these irritations were short-lived; and, during the last years of Burroughs' life, he seemed more and more preoccupied with Emerson, from whom he began to borrow titles for his own writing: *Bird and Bough*, "Journeying Atoms," "The Primal Mind," "Fated to be Free." Also, Emersonian turns of phrase and metaphors rather abruptly became much more noticeable in his later work than in his middle years; for example, these passages which are taken from a single essay, "Religion" (*Field and Study*, 1919): "Are we ourselves anything more than the tracks of the Eternal in the dust of the earth?" (242); "the morning star is no more divine than the morning earth" (243); "the Nature-God is no better than we are, and we are as good as he is, we are bone of his bone, and flesh of his flesh, mere atoms and molecules in a corporeal frame that fills and is the universe" (247).

An indication of the vigor of Burroughs' renewed interest is the fact that he read in their entirety all ten of the volumes of Emerson's *Journals* as they appeared from 1909 to 1914. One result of this reading was two articles, "Emerson and His Journals" and "Flies in Amber," totaling 102 pages in the posthumous *The Last Harvest*. A labor of love, or perhaps of religion, Burroughs begins the first of these essays with some general considerations. He speaks of the Emersonian "habit of mind" (2) that remains after the fervor of one's first youthful reading of Emerson wears off—a lifelong way of looking at the universe with faith in its "essential soundness and goodness" (2). Emerson's great contribution is that "he helps to make you feel at home in nature, and in your land and generation" (2). He enhances the value of literature, relates the material and spiritual realms of being, and demonstrates the immanence of the moral law. Emerson's poems Burroughs describes aptly as "the fruit of Oriental mysticism and bardic fervor grafted upon the shrewd, parsimonious, New England puritanic stock" (9).

Burroughs was still somewhat chilled by what he considers Emerson's coldness, his lack of true capacity for warm friendship—a failing, in Burroughs' view, of the Transcendentalists as a group—and he quotes Emerson's remark: "I like man but not men" (38); but he concedes that Emerson's passion for nature did much to make up for his coolness for people. He also appreciates Emerson's interest, aloof though it might be, in the common people, the mob and their racy speech. Above all, he is impressed by Emerson's independence of orthodoxy; and he applauds Emerson's pronouncement that "God builds his temple in the heart on the ruins of churches and religion" (48). He is equally delighted that Emerson developed no systematic dogma of his own.

In "Flies in Amber," Burroughs deplores the excessive carping at Emerson in the early twentieth century and regrets a growing neglect of him amidst the distractions of the times. How, he asks, can Emerson compete "even in university towns . . . against the 'movies' (a word so ugly [he hesitates] to write it) in the next street?" (87). Nevertheless, Burroughs again proceeds to discuss several weaknesses in Emerson. He notes the obvious disconnectedness of Emerson's paragraphs, except in some of his earliest essays. Using a geological simile, he writes that in Emerson's later work there is "nonconformity between the strata which make up his paragraphs. There is only juxtaposition" (89). Burroughs accounts for this looseness by the fact that Emerson's writings usually are transcriptions of popular lectures in which tightly logical composition would be inappropriate. Also, Burroughs finds grounds for criticism in Emerson's use of analogy—one of his favorite means of expression. Always interested in the concept of analogy, Burroughs observes that Emerson occasionally falters; for example, he cites the following quite confusing, if not meaningless, figure: "Each plant has its parasites, and each created thing its lover and poet" (94).

At the time Burroughs was taken by his final illness, he was attempting to edit "Flies in Amber," which was, and still remains, somewhat disorganized. His strength being unequal to the task, he told his friend Dr. Clara Barrus to do with it what she could. On her request that he at least write a conclusion for it, he mustered his energy and wrote the following, which proved to be the last words from his pen: "Let us keep alive the Emersonian memories: that such a man has lived and wrought among us. Let us teach our children his brave and heroic words. and plant our lives upon as secure an ethical foundation as he did. Let us make pilgrimages to Concord, and stand with uncovered heads beneath the pine tree where his ashes rest. He left us an estate in the fair land of the Ideal. He bequeathed us treasures that thieves cannot break through and steal, nor time corrupt, nor rust nor moth destroy" (102).

II   *Carlyle*

Burroughs considered Thomas Carlyle one of the major literary influences in his life. Becoming acquainted with his writing almost as early as with Emerson's, he has high praise for him in a *Saturday Press* essay of 1860: "Carlyle is so concise that his meaning heats his words to a white heat. De Quincey is sometimes so diffuse that his thought barely warms his ponderous diction. Carlyle's style creaks and groans like a loaded wagon over a rough road; De Quincey's moves with the swiftness and ordered celerity of a passenger train on velveted rails. Motion, motion, and occasionally much unoccupied room, is emphatically the characteristic of De Quincey; labor, labor, like a river wearing its channel is the prominent feature of Carlyle. Carlyle's steeds are of the sun, with manes of fire and volcanic strength, but ringboned from the colt, and choked with too tight a harness . . ." (June 23, 1860, p. 3). Burroughs' metaphors may be of a questionable mixture, but he does demonstrate that he has an ear for style. His early taste for Carlyle stayed with him and even carried him through the interminable pages of *Frederick the Great*.

Burroughs wrote frequently about Carlyle, either devoting whole essays to him or touching upon him in pieces primarily on other subjects. His most extensive treatment is "A Sunday in Cheyne Row," occupying seventy-two pages of *Fresh Fields* (1884). One of his most impressive and penetrating critical essays, it begins as a reminiscence of Burroughs' visit to Carlyle eleven years earlier, since which time Carlyle has died. Burroughs again goes to Chelsea and gazes at the old house, deserted and run down, and his thoughts wander through the whole range of the dead writer's works. His chief interest is in the Emerson-Carlyle relationship. The basic comparison that he makes between the two is that Emerson's preoccupations are with the ideal and the universal while Carlyle's are with the practical and the temporal. In his grasp of the everyday and historical affairs of man, Carlyle is incomparably the superior. Nor does Burroughs hesitate to state which ability he admires the more: "Emerson's two words were truth and beauty, which lie, as it were, in the same plane, and the passage from one to another is easy. . . . Carlyle's two words were truth and duty, which lie in quite different planes, and the passage between which is steep and rough" (223). The implication that Emerson is not concerned with duty is unjust; he himself regarded his entire ethic of self-reliance as extremely challenging to the moral powers: "If any one imagines that this law is lax, let him keep its commandments one day." Yet his major preoccupation was not with duty, with conduct, as was Carlyle's.

As Burroughs says, Carlyle was temperamentally a man of action; Emerson a man of thought. The difference between the two, superimposed on similar foundations of Transcendentalism, is what made their famous correspondence so interesting: "Emerson wants Emersonian epigrams from Carlyle, and Carlyle wants Carlylean thunder from Emerson" (225). More of a man of action himself than Emerson, Burroughs the bank examiner, the outdoorsman, the traveler, and the farmer felt closer kinship with Carlyle—but, as already noted, he loved Emerson more. The Carlyle ethic of hard work well done is everywhere apparent in Burroughs' life. Carlyle "raises aloft the standard of the individual will, the supremacy of man over events" (244).

Thus, to Burroughs, Carlyle is not a metaphysical philosopher; he is, rather, a moralist, a prophet, an indefatigable driver not only of his fellow men but of himself, as is attested by his thirteen years of lonely labor on the life of Frederick the Great, the work which Burroughs considered his greatest. Carlyle could be satisfied with nothing less than the heroic in himself and others. And since the others, the masses of mankind, are devoid of the heroic potential, he becomes a fierce opponent of democracy. Here Burroughs, the friend of Whitman, would of necessity disagree, elaborating counterarguments which will be discussed later. In any event, he sees in Carlyle a "God-burdened" (279) soul performing the part, similar to Whitman's, of a modern prophet exhorting and lashing a lax people along the road of virtue.

Included also in *Fresh Fields* is an essay of more than twenty pages called "In Carlyle's Country," an account of Burroughs' visit to

Ecclefechan, Scotland, where Carlyle was born. To Burroughs, Carlyle was in part a product of the geography and climate of his native Annandale—much as Wordsworth was of the Lake District, which Burroughs had just previously toured. The result of the Scottish visit was that Burroughs developed a strong feeling of affinity with Carlyle. To begin with, he considered himself a Celt, having a Welsh strain on his father's side and an Irish one on his mother's, and thus could claim racial ties with the Scotsman. But more important, the conditions of Carlyle's boyhood had been similar to those of Burroughs': both had been born into hard-working families of many children in a hilly country. Carlyle's father, though first a mason, was later a farmer like Burroughs' father; and both were staunch, unbending Calvinists by faith and manner of living. In all aspects of Carlyle's life and work Burroughs finds "the family stamp.... Carlyle's heart was always ... in Scotland. A vague, yearning homesickness seemed ever to possess him" (65-67), and Burroughs quotes Carlyle himself from *Past and Present*: "Mystic, deep as the world's centre, are the roots I have struck into my Native Soil; no *tree* that grows is rooted so" (*Fresh Fields*, 67). Such an attachment could strike only a sympathetic chord in Burroughs, who had like ties with his Western Catskill valley where the tilted, stone-walled fields and sweeping mountain ridges put one in mind of the Scottish countryside.

Attachments such as these, Burroughs well knew, are only deepened by the poverty, toil, and suffering that generations of Carlyles and Burroughses had endured in their ancestral hills. Even Carlyle's style, Burroughs thought, could be traced to his Annandale origins. All the Carlyles, the sexton of Ecclefechan informed Burroughs, "spoke as if against a stone wall. (Their words hit hard)" (79). Carlyle's eccentric prose was actually an echoing of his father's trade as stonemason. Burroughs rightly takes to task Taine—who of all critics should have recognized hereditary and environmental influences at work—for not tracing Carlyle's manner of writing to its familial origins.[2]

III   *Thoreau*

Among the writers who had most influenced him, Burroughs on occasion mentioned Thoreau, though at other times he denied any influence. Critical of Thoreau's weaknesses and inaccuracies as a field naturalist, he nevertheless declared that *Cape Cod* and *The Maine Woods* were the best nature books ever produced in this country. Burroughs' first important essay on Thoreau—"Henry D. Thoreau"—

was printed in the *Century Magazine* of July, 1882 (later in *Indoor Studies*, 1889). On the whole, this essay, which is among the earliest extensive and serious treatments of its subject to be printed in a major journal, is laudatory and appreciative; but it has some reservations, and as such is typical of Burroughs' critiques of Thoreau, including the last—"Another Word on Thoreau" (*The Last Harvest*, 1922; and, much shorter, as "A Critical Glance into Thoreau," *The Atlantic Monthly*, June, 1919), which was written when Burroughs was over eighty years old. Always Burroughs found Thoreau to be "first and last, a moral force speaking in the terms of the literary naturalist" (*The Last Harvest*, 113).

In his *Century* article of 1892 Burroughs states that Thoreau's nature studies, like his own, were a means to an end that was never attained. They were phases, surely the most important ones, of a lifelong search for an understanding of existence and of the universe; and, of course, though Thoreau may have come closer than most, he no more found this understanding than he found his famous hound, bay horse, and turtledove. Preeminently, Thoreau was a man devoted to principle. Burroughs dismisses the charge of an English critic that Thoreau was a skulker, nor did he share Emerson's regret that Thoreau never rose higher than the captaincy of a huckleberry party. To Burroughs, Thoreau gave the world the best that was in him, and this best was very good indeed. Yet, though his merit lay in his personal qualities as a seeker, he could, if principle demanded, enter the political arena, as when he defended John Brown in a lecture to the people of Concord. Thoreau was a skulker only "in the great army of Mammon" (*Indoor Studies*, p. 11). His gift to mankind was in the coin, not of the realm, but of character. His life was its own justification.

Thoreau's lifelong search for "wildness," both as a woodsman and as a poet-mystic, Burroughs believes, was actually a search for health—a suggestion from James Russell Lowell, perhaps, who in his essay on Thoreau states that Thoreau's "whole life was a search for the doctor."[3] Lowell's reference was, of course, to mental health; but Burroughs includes physical also. Not only did Burroughs equate Thoreau's search for wildness, but his whole existence with his search for a cure. Perhaps if one takes into account Thoreau's tendency to hypochondria—which also afflicted Burroughs—he will find Lowell closer to the truth. But, in any event, Thoreau sought the company of wild animals and primitive men, especially Indians; and, when he could not find the latter, he sought Indian arrowheads, which he found with a facility that could only result from a passionate interest. In this life, one is prone to find the things that one's innermost nature demands. So avid was Thoreau's concern with nature, the health-giver, that, as Burroughs aptly puts it, he kept her "under a sort of police surveillance the year round. ... Not a mouse or a squirrel must leave its den without his knowledge. ... He watched the approach of spring as a doctor watches the development of a critical case. He felt the pulse of the wind and the temperature of the day at all hours" (43). But Burroughs falls short of one fascinating speculation, a corollary of what he had to say about Thoreau's quest for wildness as a consequence of his invalidism. Was not Thoreau, who practiced a rigorous mortification of the flesh and refused the attendance of a physician at his deathbed, perhaps unconsciously seeking death, the ultimate absorption into nature, the ultimate cure?

Burroughs finds Thoreau's prose more expressive even than Emerson's, but he believes it directly reflects an inability to compromise. "He puts a threatening claw or beak into his paragraphs ... and feathers his shafts with the nicest art" (19). Consistently antagonistic toward any aspect of the human norm, Thoreau uses the most powerful weapon against complacency—paradox. Thus, he refused to express conventional grief at the death of his brother John; and, when Emerson's son died, he wrote to a friend, "Do not the flowers die every autumn? ... It would have been strange if [the boy] had lived" (22).

Thoreau's sentences, Burroughs points out, are as abrupt as they are honest, though their thought is frequently extravagant and shocking. He makes his statements extreme so that they will run no danger of being dull. He would do anything to awaken his reader. Thus, *Walden* "is certainly the most delicious piece of brag in literature" (33)—a statement which, without being intended as derogatory, is as true as it is irritating to those who regard *Walden* as holy scripture. Most of Thoreau's written utterance, as well as his oral, is brag and was intended to be so—for brag is irritating, and Thoreau's purpose was to irritate his fellow men into awareness. Indeed, among the Transcendentalists as a group, Burroughs detected a notable element of "tall talk"—as in Emerson's boast, "Give me health and a day, and I will make the pomp of emperors ridiculous" (172), or in much of Whitman's "Song of Myself," for example,

> My ties and ballasts leave me, my elbows rest in sea-gaps,
> I skirt sierras, my palms cover continents,
> I am afoot with my vision.

The Last Harvest, a hundred pages of which were devoted to Emerson, also includes a twenty-thousand-word essay, "Another Word on Thoreau," Burroughs' longest and most penetrating study of this author. Thoreau's most valuable contribution, Burroughs thinks, was not "a philosophy, but a life. He gave us fresh and beautiful literature, he gave us our first and probably only nature classic, he gave us an example of plain living and high thinking that is always in season, and he took upon himself that kind of noble poverty that carries the suggestion of wealth of soul" (108-9). He mentions Thoreau's admiration for John Brown, with the wildness of whose temperament something in Thoreau harmonized; and he speaks with gratitude of Thoreau's acceptance of Whitman, another free spirit, as "the greatest democrat which [sic] the world had yet seen" (111).

Again discounting Thoreau as a scientist, Burroughs describes him as "not a born naturalist, but a born supernaturalist" (134). Burroughs elaborates on what he had said in his *Century* essay concerning the humor in Thoreau's paradoxes and boastfulness. He now emphasizes that Thoreau was a humorist in the true Yankee manner—a combination of "brag" and good-natured, quizzical slyness. His way of life based on a calculated disappointment of his friends in their expectations of him especially amused Burroughs as the ultimate in downright contrariness or "cussedness." Thoreau was "too religious to go to church, too patriotic to pay his taxes, too fervent a humanist to interest himself in the social welfare of his neighborhood" (121). Thoreau was a "character," with "more crust than crumb" (121); and for this reason one notices him.

Thoreau's insistence on living as he saw fit and not as his friends and neighbors would have him doubtlessly appealed to Burroughs, who resolutely conducted his existence as he pleased. Certainly, he had more in common with Thoreau than with Emerson, for like Thoreau, he earned much of his living with his hands, was a passionate outdoorsman, and indeed had his own cabin retreat a mile or so away from his village. Most notably, perhaps, Burroughs was prompted by Thoreau's boat trip on the Merrimack and Concord Rivers to make a similar voyage on the Pepacton, or east branch of the Delaware River, which had its rise in the Grand Gorge a few miles from the home farm at Roxbury.

The essay, "Pepacton," that resulted from Burroughs' adventure differs from Thoreau's *A Week on the Concord and Merrimack Rivers* in that it is much shorter—only forty pages long, in fact—and lacks the philosophizing that Burroughs considered a blemish on Thoreau's book. Burroughs' purpose in his account was the same as Thoreau's: to convey to the reader the author's sense of wonder in familiar surroundings. But Burroughs is actually the more successful of the two in that he has capitalized on a circumstance that Thoreau overlooked. What Burroughs realized, and Thoreau did not, was that a voyage down a small stream in a rowboat is such an unusual form of travel that it immediately sets the traveler off from the rest of humanity. Farmers in their fields, boys along the bank, housewives from whom Burroughs bought milk—all experienced astonishment. A man of their own county and of their own agricultural way of life was voyaging among them and yet was not among them; he had separated himself from them as much as if he had been a visitant from a distant continent. And this astonishment is transferred to the reader. Only the boys along the route were not amazed with the traveler, and they matter-of-factly warned him of Odysseyan dangers—whirlpools, rocks, rapids. Without fanfare or didacticism, the essay neatly makes its point—that the voyage of life is full of marvels and wonders if men will take the trouble to look from a fresh viewpoint. The notion is Thoreauvian; and Burroughs' debt to Thoreau for it must be recorded, since it exemplifies the similarity of their temperaments in many respects.

In spite of this and other indebtedness, there were important differences between the two. Burroughs, with his Washington experience and his foreign travels, broke away from the parochialism that Thoreau considered a virtue; but Burroughs' attachment to the Catskills and his boyhood farm was probably as passionate as Thoreau's for Concord. More importantly, Burroughs, unlike Thoreau and even Emerson, sought, enjoyed, and admittedly needed, friendship and social intercourse. "Need a nature-lover ... necessarily be a man-hater?" (123), Burroughs asks apropos of Thoreau. Need individualism be nurtured to the exclusion of all altruism? To both questions Burroughs answers an emphatic, *No*; but Thoreau answers, *Yes*, whether with tongue in cheek or not. The extreme individualism of all the New England Transcendentalists, including Emerson, struck Burroughs as lacking in the human warmth that was the crowning trait of Whitman's character. Burroughs also finds something disingenuous in Thoreau's professed scorn of all civilization, for it was precisely this same civilization that provided him with his means of livelihood—surveying, lecturing, writing—and which afforded him the education at Harvard College and the perspective necessary for the very existence of his idealistic and primitivistic opinions. Granted that "Thoreau's life was a search for the wild" (127), the starting point for such a search would have to have been some such highly civilized area as New England.

Though generally favorable, the essay on Thoreau in *The Last Harvest* is somewhat more critical than the one published forty years earlier in the *Century*. In the later article Burroughs expresses admiration for Thoreau's prose style at its best, when it is sheer poetry; but he carps at frequent false analogies which Thoreau allows to slip into his writing. "Most poems," writes Thoreau, "like the fruits, are sweetest toward the blossom end"—but, asks Burroughs, "which *is* the blossom end of a poem?" (142). Or, in an even more cryptic statement, "The poet must sustain his body by his poetry, as a steam planing-mill feeds its boilers with the shavings it makes" (144), one finds it impossible to straighten out the analogy.

Again Burroughs touches upon Thoreau's "tall talk," but a little less approvingly, as well as on other stylistic and personal idiosyncrasies. He enjoys picking several extreme and contrary statements and commenting on them. When Thoreau asserts that a humming mosquito is to him the equal of Homer, Burroughs wonders "what he would have made of a blow-fly buzzing on the pane" (143). And Burroughs is a little skeptical when Thoreau assures us that "the dry wit of decayed cranberry leaves, and the fresh Attic salt of the moss-beds" are more informative and inspiring than "a day passed in the society of those Greek sages ... as described in the Banquet of Xenophon" (144); or when Thoreau blusters that he "would not go around the corner to see the world blow up" (142). Burroughs quotes Emerson to the effect that the secret of Thoreau's style was to use the unexpected—whether thought or phrase or word: "If I were sadder, I should be happier." "The longer I have forgotten you, the more I remember you" (141-42). Burroughs thinks such paradoxes can be pleasing if used with discretion—as when Thoreau writes, "I like his looks and the sound of his silence" (142)—but they can become objectionable if used carelessly or for mere shock effect in apparent disregard of meaning.

Finally, Burroughs questions the purpose of much of Thoreau's diary, the fourteen volumes of which appear to him as the monument to a life-consuming obsession. Much of the content of the *Journal* is, Burroughs admits, significant and was useful to its author as a source for his other writings. But vast tracts are merely the dumping ground for worthless details: the ring counts and stump measurements of all the trees in a recently cut woodlot; the depth of snow every tenth step during a winter's tramp; pages of description of the perfectly normal behavior of a kitten; and lists of the Latin names of weeds. This craving for "exact but useless facts" Burroughs brands as "abnormal" (152), as any strong compulsion doubtlessly is.

Rather convincingly, Burroughs argues that a markedly neurotic element existed in Thoreau's personality. Aside from his compulsiveness, Burroughs points out that Thoreau's real or feigned misanthropy—which took the form of a fear of being sullied by men in their everyday affairs—stemmed from a dearth of self-respect. Even Emerson, Burroughs points out, remarked on Thoreau's tiresome irritability and hostility—sure signs of deep-seated insecurity. Yet Burroughs does not dwell on these peculiarities or present them as pejorative to Thoreau's position as America's greatest nature writer. For, above and beyond any eccentricities, there is Thoreau's consummate idealism—his insistence on getting one's "living by loving" (163)—by working for the pleasure of one's occupation rather than for money or bread. "There has been but one Thoreau," Burroughs concludes, "and we should devoutly thank the Gods of New England for the precious gift" (170).

IV   *Esthetic Theory: Science and Poetry*

Burroughs wrote rather extensive criticisms of other writers—notably of Wordsworth, Matthew Arnold, and Gilbert White—whom he admired highly. Altogether, his critical writing would fill four or five volumes; it is of such generally high quality that the fact that it has been all but overlooked is inexplicable. Although Burroughs' fame as a nature essayist eclipsed his reputation as a critic, the editors of the leading periodicals and publishing houses of the day respected him as a critic and sought his essays for magazines and as introductions to editions of standard works; these in turn were read by numerous educated and presumably intelligent readers whose tastes and literary enthusiasms they must have influenced. Of other literary critics of the sixty years during which Burroughs wrote, only Lowell was perhaps his equal in quality but not in continuance or in breadth of interest or influence. Howells certainly must be considered, but his enthusiasms ran to fiction, especially that of foreign countries—interests more restricted than Burroughs'.

In addition to criticism of individual authors, Burroughs developed an esthetic theory. From the very start of his literary career, he sought a definition of poetry—by which he meant imaginative literature in general, including the prose essay. Irresistibly drawn to literature, he wished an understanding, satisfactory for himself at least, of what interested him. He was also attracted by science, and he wished to understand its difference from literature, for he felt there was much that was incompatible between the two though they assuredly were not entirely unrelated. His thought on literature reached its fullest and most mature expression in the essays in *Literary Values*, published in 1902, when he himself was sixty-five years of age. But for over forty years previously he had been thinking about the subject and regularly recording his thoughts, and the particularly rich repositories of them are *Birds and Poets* (1877) and *Indoor Studies* (1889).

His first essay on the subject, "Poetry," appeared in the *Saturday Press* of November 3, 1860. In germ, it contains the ideas basic to most of what he later wrote about esthetics: "Poetry is that part of Literature that lies nearest to life; it is in fact life articulate. . . . Poetry need leave nothing out, should never skip and affect a girlish prudishness. No object is beneath the art of a master. Paint truly, that's the secret; not accurately, that is the business of science; but give the object as it seems, as it represents itself to our moods and feelings, as it stands related to our life. . . . Poetry is Life speaking, and therefore, should give things not as they are in themselves, but as they are in our experience" (3).

Burroughs' friendship with Whitman also motivated much of his speculation about poetry. Burroughs' thoughts on the nature of genius and beauty, as developed in the essays "Before Genius" and "Before Beauty," were directed primarily at revealing the source of Whitman's achievement—a deep and unconscious kinship with nature. Elsewhere in the same volume in which these appeared, *Birds and Poets*, he reemphasizes and expands the fundamental proposition that "the true poet knows more about Nature than the naturalist because he carries her open secrets in his heart" (58). Thus, it matters little whether the writer be a celebrator of the city, like Charles Lamb, or of the country, like Thoreau, or of both, like Whitman; for nature exists among the urban throngs as well as in the primeval forest; and the poet, her devotee and priest, will find her in either place. The poet indeed is himself a natural phenomenon, and his poetry has its being in "the vital fluids, the bowels, the chest, the appetites, and is to be read and judged only through love and compassion" (61). Poets must enter into their subjects "through their blood, their sexuality and manliness, instead of standing apart and criticising them and writing *about* them through mere intellectual cleverness and 'smartness' " (62).

In two pieces in *Pepacton* (1881)–"Nature and the Poets" and the last of the "Notes by the Way," a collection of short observations—Burroughs discusses the deplorable incidence of inaccuracies among the standard poets in their treatment of natural phenomena. He is willing to grant poetic license, and he is aware, and happy, that the poet is not a scientist: "The poet himself does not so much read in Nature's book—though he does this, too—as write his own thoughts there. Nature needs him, she is the page and he the type, and she takes the impression he gives" (125). However, Burroughs believes the artist should be in command of the facts. Shakespeare, on whose accuracy of observation he comments in "Notes by the Way," receives the highest rating, though even he can slip, as when, accepting an error of the times, he speaks of a hive of bees as a kingdom (*Henry V*). Among the American poets, Emerson and Whittier err the least and Longfellow the most, partly because he confuses American and European nature. But Whitman surpasses them all in his knowledge (gained with Burroughs' help) of the facts of nature and uses them most cautiously and hence most felicitously. Among the lines of Whitman that he quotes as models of acute observation are: "The vitreous pour of the full moon just tinged with blue"; "The slender and jagged threads of lightning, as sudden and fast amid the din they chased each other across the sky."

Among later British poets Wordsworth—who appeals to Burroughs more than any other English poet—is outstanding for his fidelity to the nature that he knew and experienced. His poetry is, consequently, saturated with the spirit of the Westmoreland countryside. But paradoxically—and this is what makes Wordsworth great—he is not solely or primarily a poet of nature: "He is more the poet of man, deeply wrought upon by a certain phase of nature—the nature of those sombre, quiet, green, far-reaching mountain solitudes" (*Fresh Fields*, 164). Nor does Burroughs simply mean that Wordsworth was the poet of shepherds and villagers but of himself as a child, a product of the hills: "He brooded upon nature, but it was nature mirrored in his own heart" (164-65)—the only way a poet *should* write about nature. In nature accurately observed, man, even if he is a scientist, sees himself: this was an elemental truth to Burroughs. Hence, in an attempt to define realism, Burroughs rejects photographylike transcriptions as art. Literature must provide a pathway from the world of actuality to the world of the ideal—which is an inner world. The artists must start with the concrete, but the source of all true art is the soul of the artist and the soul of his audience. The real must be infused with passion and emotion before it can command the esthetic interests of mankind; therefore, "Paradoxical as it may seem, it is only the idealist who can adequately deal with the real . . ." (*Indoor Studies*, 255).

V   *Esthetic Theory:* Literary Values

Burroughs' fullest statement of his esthetic theory is in *Literary Values* (1902). Though much that he presents in it had already been developed in earlier writings, it also contains much that is new. In addition, it reflects a change that had come over Burroughs' thought. With increasing years he had become more objective, more capable of constructive criticism even of such favorites as Whitman and Emerson, as well as more Classical in his outlook. His rather tepid previous admiration for Matthew Arnold, whose Hellenism he had believed placed too much emphasis on the mind as opposed to the heart, had increased, as had the number of quotations from Arnold's work.

The title essay of *Literary Values*, originally published in the *Century* of April, 1902, sets the tone for the collection, which is more closely unified in theme than most of Burroughs' books. The purpose is the Arnoldian one of discovering a set of standards, of *values*, by which one can recognize a true work of literary art. Burroughs has asked himself the question as to why one literary work passes into quick oblivion and another outlasts its own and later generations. The enduring work clearly must have qualities that the ephemeral one lacks; and these qualities, he concludes, are the "staple, fundamental human virtues . . . probity, directness, simplicity, sincerity, love" (5). A writer like Isaak Walton, Daniel Defoe, or John Bunyan, whose style has these qualities, has a much better chance of survival than a writer like Carlyle or Robert Browning, whose style is affected, eccentric, obscure, or self-conscious. Complete seriousness and honesty, with no exhibitionism, are what ultimately count. The author's utterance must be as much from his heart as are the utterances of peasants and workers, whose speech often has high literary value. At all events, a striving for the frills of learning and culture can result only in artificiality that may delight for a day but no longer.

Yet Burroughs admits that there is a magic that enters into style. So often the effectiveness of a sentence or of a line of poetry depends on one word, and Burroughs quotes different versions of verses by Keats and Poe to prove his point: "A thing of beauty is a continual joy"—as Keats first wrote his famous line—is surely inferior to his later, "A thing of beauty is a joy forever"; and it is not the more regular meter of the latter that is decisive. Nor would anyone argue that Poe's first phrasing, "To the beauty of fair Greece,/ And the grandeur of old Rome," though metrically perfect, is not feeble in comparison to his final, "To the glory that was Greece,/ And the grandeur that was Rome" (13-14). One can argue that, in the case of Poe, alliteration accounts for the superiority of the second version; yet alliteration can just as well be a detriment as an asset.

Even more intangible than phrasing, and yet of equal importance as a source of value, is the manner in which style conveys a sense of an author's personality. What interests the reader most in a novel by Hawthorne, for example? Is it the plot, the characters, or Hawthorne himself as revealed by all these but mainly by style? Burroughs believes that Hawthorne himself draws a reader to his pages. The same stories in the same settings with the same characters would affect one much differently if written by another. Fiction, of course, does have much to offer in addition to style; but action and characterization, suspense, and structure—indispensable though they may be—are as nothing in comparison with the manner of narration, the author's style and his personality as conveyed by it. In a way, style is the receptacle of the vital principle that makes a book live from generation to generation. Burroughs applies the theory of evolution to literary survival: "the struggle for existence goes on in the ideal world as well as in the real. The strongest mind, the fittest statement, survives . . ." (18). The most vigorous intellect or imagination, equipped with the greatest skill in translating itself into literary expression, enjoys the longest life.

In another essay, "Style and the Man," in *Literary Values*, Burroughs further explores the relationship of style and personality; and he concludes that the two are inseparable, that style is the man. By one of his favorite analogies he compares an author—who creates works of art by mingling the raw material of life and nature with the quality of his own character, mind, and imagination—to a bee, which by an inner chemistry transforms sweet water from a flower into honey. One reads Thoreau, for example, not for what he says about nature but for what his treatment of nature says about him. Another author working with the same material would produce an entirely different effect, for style cannot be imitated. A work, then, is not great because of the greatness of its subject but because of the greatness of its author: "All pure literature is the revelation of a man" (65).

An example of how Burroughs applies his ideas on style to a specific author is found in his essay "Matthew Arnold's Criticism" in *Indoor*

Studies. A strength that Arnold derived from his Hellenism—so much a part of his character and intellectual makeup—was his literary style, which Burroughs considers preeminent among writers of English prose in the nineteenth century. This admiration was genuine on Burroughs' part, and his own prose—once the Emerson influence was mostly shaken off—generally resembled Arnold's more than that of any other author, British or American. Noting "the unity, transparency, centrality of Arnold's mind" (132), Burroughs finds these qualities reflected in their possessor's prose, which "is like cut glass . . . not merely clear," having "a distinction, a prestige, which belongs to it by reason of its delicate individuality . . ." (133). Lacking purple patches, Arnold's writing is not an end in itself; rather, it is a means to lucid, integral, and consecutive expression. In short, it is a reflection of Arnold's own mind, which is what holds the reader of Arnold.

Didacticism or utility as dominant purposes are foreign to pure literature. In another essay in *Literary Values*, "Thou Shalt Not Preach," written under the negative influence of Tolstoy's *What Is Art?*, Burroughs takes issue with the great Russian, whom he otherwise revered. Literature not only may but must exist for its own sake; a poet is neither physician nor preacher, but a creator of beauty out of the special quality of his mind and soul in contact with the outer world. Since a writer creates beauty with words, his own unduplicatable way of dealing with words—that is, his style—is the all-important indication of the quality of his creation.

But style, of course, must be spontaneous; it cannot be labored or self-conscious; the writer should think constantly of what he wishes to say, not how he will say it. Ideas should come first—even though they are not the most important final product of a piece of writing—and words should follow, but naturally and unaffectedly. Burroughs quotes Whitman against meddling with art by straining to be "literary" or original (74). Swinburne is a prime example of how not to write, for his poems contain "such a din and echo of rhyme and alliteration that it is almost impossible to hear what the man is really saying" (74). The best writers offer no such "friction" (77). In prose, Meredith and Henry James are almost as reprehensible to Burroughs as Swinburne is in verse.

In another essay, "Lucid Literature," Burroughs reemphasizes his conviction of the indispensability of absolute clarity of style. Yet he does not always demand direct statement; he places high value on suggestion, which is the subject of still another essay in the volume; for suggestion draws from the reader what he himself brings to a work—a process which is always an important part of a reader's enjoyment. But suggestion is far from synonymous with obscurity. Likewise, Burroughs does not exclude eloquence of the type found in Edward Gibbon and Tacitus. Such authors afford real pleasure through their rhetoric, though their style falls short of the poetic as exemplified in much of the prose of Emerson and Carlyle, in whom "the sonorous ring" (179) of Gibbon is absent but the imagination is active. Prose, of course, may be poetic; and poetry may be eloquent, rather than poetic, as in much of Byron and in almost all patriotic verse.

As for Burroughs' style, he was concerned with it without being self-conscious about it, except very early when he was trying to discard its Emersonian qualities. He had acquired his distinctive personal manner as early as 1865 in his nature essays for the *Atlantic*, which were later published in *Wake-Robin*. He had indeed developed a remarkable literary tool, one which merited the comment in the *Westminster Review* that language in his hands "is like a violin in the hands of a master."[4] At the same time, Burroughs disclaims any great facility, saying he can "only walk along a straight, smooth path."[5] He elsewhere avows that all he does is write about things as they have impinged on his senses—telling of them exactly as they are to him. Yet he makes no pretense at being an effortless writer, for whatever effectiveness his prose may have is the result of hard, unremitting labor. But the labor is not directed toward the *achieving* of a style; the style comes automatically as a by-product of the hard work. His constant effort has been to vitalize his writings, to get beneath the surface chaff of random words, and to transfer to his sentences his own feeling of the life and reality of his subject. Sometimes poetry results—that is, prose with poetic elements; but such poetry forms by itself in the unconscious mind under the stimulus of the senses and issues forth in the quiet retrospection of writing in a diary or in an essay.

In *Literary Values*, Burroughs considers the concept of style to be inclusive of many qualities that lend value to writing: it is the vehicle of the author's character; when effective, it brings a piece of literature to life; and it controls the reader's response to the subject matter of what he is reading. But there are other literary values than style, and among these is the inclusion or transmission of moral sense. Burroughs considers this function of extreme importance, for he believes the moral sense to be more highly developed in democratic societies of the modern world than in any other time or culture. Especially notable is this development among the Nordic peoples; the modern Latins, like the ancient Greeks, excel in art rather than in virtue, though Burroughs in no way implies that they are entirely lacking in that quality. Thus, Poe, who stresses the esthetic rather than the moral, has never been held in so high esteem in America as in France. Americans prefer Whittier, though he is a much inferior artist. An appeal to the moral and spiritual faculties of man, even if coupled with relatively crude or unpolished art, as with Emerson and Wordsworth, is more poetic—at least to the Anglo-Saxon mind—than the perfect art of Tennyson, Swinburne, or Gustave Flaubert. Burroughs cautions, nevertheless, that this moral quality must not be confused with didacticism; it is, rather, the poet's "profound . . . emotion when in the presence of simple common things" (22), as Burroughs says of Wordsworth. "The great artist . . . is primarily in love with life and things, and not with art" (23-24).

In "Democracy and Literature" (*Literary Values*), Burroughs attempts to define the function of literature. Literary values, he believes, do not change radically from one society or era to another, but the emphases shift and the vehicles of these values differ. Any social order will probably produce a quota of superior literary minds comparable to that of any other. Democratic institutions thus need not entail a degradation of standards so far as genius is concerned, but they must entail a raising of the standards of the masses. As for shifts of emphasis, Burroughs cites Whitman and Tolstoy—to him the two most outstanding examplars of the democratic spirit in literature—as having extended the religious outlook to include all mankind as sons of God. Whitman has accomplished this through his Transcendentalism; Tolstoy, through his primitive Christianity with its focus upon the meek and the lowly. No longer are the Calvinistic elect or the divine-right aristocrats under a special favor of God; for the realm of the spirit, as revealed in literature, embraces equally all men.

With the refocusing of the older religious views comes a greater concern for the welfare of the poor and downtrodden; letters become more humanitarian as well as humane; and goodness, honesty, sincerity, and love still remain the great values, literary as well as philosophical and religious. But these values now must find a more varied and a broader embodiment. The great virtues reside not only in noblemen and saints but in peasants and laborers. Beauty resides not only in palaces, cathedrals, and soaring mountain ranges, but in the meal in the pan and the butter in the firkin, in cottages and slums and meadows and market places. Burroughs quotes Goethe as saying that any object can become poetical—a purveyor of literary and moral value—if treated poetically (172). A railroad train can be the subject of great poetry, even though the train is essentially ugly. All of industrial and urban life can, and must, be made the subjects of poetry. "If Dante made poetry out of hell, would not a nature copious and powerful enough make poetry out of the vast and varied elements of our materialistic civilization?" (175).

Burroughs, of course, believed that Whitman, who is always the inspiration of much of his theory, has achieved just this poetic incarnation of his era and environment. Adherence to the beautiful only is no longer permissible in writing of the first quality, Burroughs points out in the essay "Mere Literature" (*Literary Values*), a title which alludes to writing which is concerned only with beauty. He has said elsewhere and repeats here that the nonbeautiful goes hand in hand with the beautiful and can no more be excluded from significant literature of the nineteenth century than can moral and social and religious considerations.

VI   *Criticism: "An art, and not a science"*

The function of the critic, as Burroughs describes it in the essay "Criticism and the Man" in *Literary Values*, is to bring living works of merit to the attention of the reader. Criticism may be descriptive, analytical, interpretive, and judicial; or, as is frequently the case, it may be two or more of these sumultaneously. As for what a criticism of Whitman's work should do, "it will describe it and analyze it, and name it as lyric, epic, dramatic, etc.; it will interpret it, or draw out and expound the ideas that lie back of it and out of which it sprang; it will seek to understand it and to get at the writer's point of view; then it will judge it, try it by its own standards, and seek to estimate the value of these standards as they stand related to the best aims and achievements of the human mind" (90-91). Such is the multipurposed function of criticism. But the critic's judicial role is paramount. He must pass judgment; and, in doing so, he must consider the personal flavor imparted to the work by the artist himself; for this personality is really the only new element—and, as has been seen, the most important one—that the artist can contribute. His function is to revitalize the old facts and verities, and the critic's duty is to estimate the artist's success in this function. He must also, however, assess the value of a work by absolute standards of esthetics and ethics. Burroughs takes issue with Howells' statement in *Criticism and Fiction* that the best critic does not praise or blame but classifies and describes (92).

Yet criticism itself, like art, is and must ultimately be self-expression. It is impossible for a critic to be purely objective; and indeed, to Burroughs, the modern temper of individualism does not demand that he be so. Criticism is, and should be, impressionistic: "Are we not coming more and more to demand that in all literary and artistic productions, the producer be present in his work, not merely as mind, as pure intelligence, but also as a distinct personality, giving a flavor of his own to the principles he utters?" (97). The affirmative answer applies to the critic as well as to the creative artist. The personal element in criticism is, in fact, usually as important a contribution as the analysis and assessment of the work under consideration. Criticism is thus "an art, and not a science" (102). "Truth plus a man" (105) makes criticism as well as literature; for criticism is indeed literature. A great critic, then, is "a great mind that finds complete self-expression in and through the works of other men" (107).

Noting the recent concern with criticism on the part of such men as Howells and Ferdinand Brunetière and especially among a host of academic writers in America, Burroughs explores in another essay in *Literary Values*, "Recent Phases of Literary Criticism," the standards of criticism in democratic societies. To begin with, he agrees heartily with Professor O. L. Triggs in rejecting absolute standards founded on an aristocratic and formalistic tradition. In a democracy, the emphasis should be on the individualism and the vitality evidenced in a work. This view would seemingly rule out Arnold and Brunetière, both upholders of an absolutism in esthetics; but Burroughs still values them; they represent something that commands respect, as does any true aristocracy. For both, and especially for Arnold, Burroughs has too high a regard to ignore them entirely. Insofar as democracy encourages barbarism and vulgarity as against fitness and good taste based on the natural and the true, Burroughs favors the standards—though, of course, not the rigidly traditional ones—of the "aristocratic critics." The trouble with Arnold and Brunetière is that their standards, while admirable, are too exclusive; they afford too little play to the personal and invidual—always desiderata for Burroughs—in literature.

VII   *Literature in the Schools*

The position of the teacher of literature is somewhat more anomalous than that of the critic, whose function, as has been seen, can be rather clearly defined. Literature, Burroughs believes, is as difficult to teach as religion. One may teach theology, but it has little to do with the development of a religious sense in the pupil. Similarly, one can analyze a literary work—its imagery, diction, sentence structure, form—but such analysis does not convey the force of the author's mind as expressed in the work. One can get into tune with an author only through sympathy and appreciation—neither of which Burroughs thinks can be taught, and he speaks from sad experience. Burroughs' own first introduction to Milton's *Paradise Lost*, for example, was through parsing its sentences—a case not so extreme as it may seem to be when one remembers the approach to poetry, especially the modern, in literature classes today. By the time the analysis is finished the poem as a whole is pretty well lost sight of. Such piecemeal treatments of a poem, Burroughs strongly felt, destroy the enjoyment of it as literature and block its legitimate function of heightening the reader's love and understanding of life. Burroughs especially deplores the parasitism of scholars who attach themselves to an author and multiply "studies" of him in disregard of the author's sole worthwhile value—his ability to convey to humanity his own deep sense of life. Such an author is, of course, Shakespeare, about whom the tonnage of books and papers almost forces one to regret that the bard ever lived. One wonders, however, if Burroughs in his repeated studies and criticisms of Whitman, and perhaps of Emerson, was not guilty of the same sin he assails.

What, then, according to Burroughs is the function of a teacher of literature? The answer is that the teacher must address himself to cultivating the tastes of his students by leading them to the best that has been written and by helping the students distinguish between the good and the second-rate. That is, he must teach discrimination between the affected, the strained, the essentially dishonest, on the one hand, and the simple, honest, direct, and natural on the other. As a minor, though specific, example of what he means, Burroughs quotes a sentence from Maurice Hewlett, a lesser British author: "In the milk of October dawns her calm brows had been dipped" (*Literary Values*, 29). Such a sentence is dishonest: it strives too hard for originality; it is unpleasant and unnatural. True, the fault seems only in the style—in the selection of images and in the sentence structure; but to Burroughs, it must be remembered, style includes many things, among them moral values. Insincere writing reflects an insincere author and sours whatever worth his work may have.

Burroughs had no intention of deemphasizing the study of literature. In *Indoor Studies* (1889) he summarily rejected the hue and cry of the times that literature be supplanted in the schools by science. The great and vital ages of the past, he is certain, have been literary rather than scientific. The study of great books with their revelation of the potentials of human character and spirit is of much surer educative value than the study of science. Literature appeals to and educates not only the intellect, but the emotions, the conscience, and the intuitions; but science educates only the intellect. In fact, science is most beneficially influential when it takes on a literary quality—is mingled with humanism—as in the works of Charles Darwin and Friedrich Humboldt. Unmodified by the humanizing spirit, science threatens to mechanize the soul—becomes a mere end in itself—with no reference to the wants of the spirit or of the heart wherein lies the true life of man. Paradoxically, literature rather than science fulfills man's acute spiritual need to feel a proximity to nature, in which "we live and move and have our being" (71): for literature presents living nature; science presents stuffed and dissected specimens in a museum showcase.

VIII   *Burroughs in the Schools*

In 1887 some of Burroughs' own writing began to be used in schools in much the way that he had recommended for literature in general. An imaginative teacher, Mary E. Burt, in the Chicago school system had convinced the Board of Education to purchase three dozen copies of *Pepacton* for her sixth-grade reading classes. The children took enthusiastically to their new book. She felt that with their background of grinding, noisy, chaotic city living they would benefit from "the tonic of a quiet literature rather than the stimulant of a stormy or dramatic one."[6] Apparently the children felt so too, for they identified with the animals described in the essays in the book and learned about meadows, brooks, and woods which they seldom if ever saw in their daily existence.

So successful was the experiment that Mr. Houghton of Houghton, Mifflin, and Company, which had published most of Burroughs' books to this time, traveled to Chicago; sensed the potential profit that might accrue from Miss Burt's novel ideas; and engaged her to edit a text specifically for classroom use. The result was a slender volume, *Birds and Bees*, which contains four rather typical selections from Burroughs' nature writing. In her introduction Miss Burt explains that the essays, as they came from their author's pen, are eminently suitable sixth-grade reading. In general, the sentences are simply constructed and the diction is not difficult. A few somewhat unusual words she defines and pronounces for the children before they begin their assignment, but in general any unfamiliar word is adequately explained by its context. As much as possible she refrains from intervening between the reader and the author. The pupils, she knows, get along very well without her interference. The next year Houghton, Mifflin published another volume, *Sharp Eyes and Other Papers*, as a school text; and it was followed by others, the last in 1923.

Thus, generation after generation of schoolchildren, over a period of at least fifty years, were introduced to Burroughs in their reading lessons; and this use helped to make him a household name. In his later years on his travels about the country, children often gathered to welcome him, and a number of schools from coast to coast were named after him. Surely no one could quarrel with this use of Burroughs' writing, for his prose does provide an exceptionally felicitous model for English expression; the development of his thoughts is logical and clear; his descriptions of birds and animals in their natural habitats are vivid and instructive. Clara Barrus claims that with this vogue for Burroughs in the classroom began a "movement of the study of nature in home and school."[7] At the very least, he helped to popularize the study of nature, and thus must rank high among those who strove to make Americans aware of the wonders and beauties that were to be enjoyed among their nation's farmlands and mountains and forests—even at their very doorsteps, if they would but take the trouble to open their eyes and look.

Today Burroughs is remembered almost exclusively as a nature writer, a naturalist. His memory persists and is revered among bird watchers and similar groups, as it should be. But Burroughs had other interests, on which he wrote as voluminously and as perceptively as on outdoor nature. If he persuaded a part of the American public to appreciate their natural environment and induced a few actually to do something toward saving this loveliness, he also—more by bludgeoning than by cajoling—awoke them to the greatness of Whitman, the sole poet of world stature their nation had produced before 1900, and strove to keep alive among us the memory and influence of others of our finest authors. And finally as a writer on the sciences—especially in biology—when they were developing with confusing rapidity, he played a useful and influential role, especially in his unwavering insistence on the continuing priority of humanistic over scientific values.

CHAPTER 4

Nature and Travel Writing

I Wake-Robin

BURROUGHS' series of sketches "From the Back Country," published in the New York *Leader* in 1861 and 1862, was the beginning of sixty years of writing about outdoor subjects. These earliest pieces already show great promise, for they are accurate in detail; they catch the spirit of the activities and the atmosphere of the places described; and they contain enough emotional undercurrent, in the form of the author's nostalgia for his native hills, to play pleasantly upon the reader's feelings. They are competent but undistinguished performances in a genre in which Burroughs only a year or two later was to excel. What stimulated him to achieve excellence was his homesickness. In an introduction to the Riverside Edition (1895) of his complete works to that time, he describes the circumstances in which he wrote *Wake-Robin* thirty years earlier while he had held a government clerkship: writing it "enabled me to live over again the days I had passed with the birds and in the scenes of my youth. I wrote the book sitting at a desk in front of an iron wall. I was the keeper of a vault in which many millions of bank-notes were stored. . . . How my mind reacted from the iron wall in front of me, and sought solace in memories of the birds and of summer fields and woods!" (Riverby Edition, Vol. I, p. xiii)

Most of the material in *Wake-Robin* had previously appeared as essays in magazines like *Putnam's* and the *Atlantic Monthly*. The title of the book—Whitman had suggested it—is the popular name for the white trillium, the flowering of which in the early spring coincides with the arrival of the birds and suggests the awakening of all nature. In his preface, Burroughs describes the book as "an invitation to the study of Ornithology," but he states that his main desire is to stimulate his readers to develop an interest in nature.

That Burroughs writes mainly—though by no means entirely—about birds in *Wake-Robin* reflects a personal enthusiasm that can be traced far back into his childhood. He reports that at the age of seven or eight he had been strangely thrilled by a glimpse of a black-throated blue warbler in the woods near his old home. Another memory from his youth was that of the cloudlike flocks of passenger pigeons that flew over the farm in the migrating seasons. The interest in birds lay dormant, however, until 1863, when he first ran across John Audubon's works in the library of the Military Academy at West Point, near which he was teaching. This first contact with the great ornithologist's writing and painting was, in Burroughs' words, "like bringing together fire and powder!"[1] Being in excellent bird country, he took at once to the fields and forest. " 'Just think of it!' he said . . . in later years, 'while the battle of Gettysburg was being fought, I was in the woods studying the birds!' "[2] But such considerations did not dampen his ardor. He pursued his interest the rest of his life and certainly became the best known, if not the most scientific, of American ornithologists. At first, he did not hesitate to shoot a specimen he wished to verify. Some of these he mounted and assembled in a glass case so tastefully that Whitman said the exhibit was a poem. But he ceased before long to carry a gun and expressed displeasure with collections of dead birds.

Wake-Robin was well received both in America and in England for its freshness and charm. Helen Hunt in *Century Illustrated Magazine* saw in it a restorative for sick spirits; Howells in the *Atlantic* applauded it for the grace and simplicity of its style and its "subtle observation."[3] Professor Dowden of Dublin, whose friendship with Burroughs was based on their admiration for Whitman, wrote that he found in *Wake-Robin* "a sense of life and growth and secret nourishment . . . so genuine, even at second hand. . . . Virtue proceeds out of anything so real, so faithful, and affectionate."[4] Burroughs had produced a minor classic, an outdoor book to be placed beside the volumes of John Muir, Richard Jefferies, or Gilbert White, to whose *The Natural History of Selborne* it has often been compared.

There are, indeed, many great merits in *Wake-Robin* which one need not discuss; but two demand attention. The reviewers without exception had dwelt upon its wholesomeness, its cheering qualities, one describing it as the "best summer book yet seen."[5] Nevertheless, a strength of the volume is that it is not entirely a summer book. Burroughs, either at this time or at any other, was under no illusions as to the universal benevolence of nature; a sentimental optimism about the general order of things never appears in his pages. Not overlooking the Edenic beauty of nature, Burroughs did not overlook the serpent that intrudes into it. For example, his description in the first essay, "The Return of the Birds," of a snake's attack on a catbird's nest quite literally, as well as chillingly, introduces the reptile into the Garden: "Three or four yards from me was the nest, beneath which, in long festoons, rested a huge black snake; a bird two thirds grown was slowly disappearing between his expanded jaws. As he seemed unconscious of my presence, I quietly observed the proceedings. By slow degrees he compassed the bird about with his elastic mouth; his head flattened, his neck writhed and swelled, and two or three undulatory movements of his glistening body finished the work. . . . I could but admire his terrible beauty . . ." (31-32). The account, brilliant in its representation of movement, continues for more than two pages, describing the terror and despair of the parent birds, until Burroughs brought the snake "looping and writhing to the ground" (34) with a well-thrown stone.

This instance illustrates how far Burroughs usually was from being the completely objective scientist; for, in moral and esthetic revulsion against the perfectly natural actions of the snake, he intervened in nature's order and attempted to impose upon it his own human sense of fitness and justice. A parallel instance is his destruction of a baby cowbird, which, as a result of that species' habit of laying its eggs in other birds' nests, was devouring all the food that a Canada warbler was bringing for its own much smaller young. "Taking the interloper by the nape of the neck, I deliberately drop it into the water, but not without a pang, as I see its naked form, convulsed with chills, float downstream. Cruel? So is Nature cruel. I take one life to save two. In less than two days this potbellied intruder would have caused the death of the two rightful occupants of the nest; so I step in and turn things into their proper channel again" (63).

Burroughs' consternation at some of nature's ways is perfectly illustrated by his feelings about buzzards. Circling and gliding effortlessly high up in the sky, these birds filled him with admiration. But one evening deep in the woods near Rock Creek in Washington he came upon the roosting place of multitudes of "the loathsome" (147) fowls. As they came beating in in the twilight until they filled the trees, their flapping wings and cowlike snortings inspired him with terror. Again attempting to rectify one of nature's apparent mistakes, he lit a fire and scared them away. Why is it that scavengers and carrion eaters are endowed such grace of slow-wheeling flight high in the summer skies?

The final essay in *Wake-Robin*, "The Invitation," restates the general purpose of the whole book, as well as of most of Burroughs' later outdoor writing, which is to invite people to open their eyes and behold the wonders that surround them, not only in the forests and mountains and remote farmlands, but in the outskirts and even in the parks of the cities. He wishes his fellow countrymen to share in the "revelation" of the beauties and wonders of nature that came to him in his boyhood and had fascinated him ever since. What he provides in this and other books is a sampler of the pleasures—and on occasion terrors—awaiting the alert observer. Like Thoreau, he is issuing a summons, though a somewhat less peremptory one, to awake.

II Winter Sunshine

Wake-Robin was followed in 1875 by *Winter Sunshine*, another volume of nature pieces on the American scene, plus a hundred pages of narrative and sketches derived from a trip that Burroughs took to England and France. The travel material is discussed elsewhere in this study, and the essays on American subjects are much the same as in *Wake-Robin* with a seasonal difference: "He who marvels at the beauty of the world in summer will find equal cause for wonder and admiration in winter. It is true the pomp and pageantry are swept away, but the essential elements remain,—the day and the night, the mountain and the valley, the elemental play and succession and the perpetual presence of the infinite sky" (47). There is one noticeable development, however, in *Winter Sunshine*: Burroughs' increasing preoccupation with human life as well as with that of the birds and beasts. In the writing about England, this change is especially apparent; but it is found in the other essays. Extremely interesting is his description in the title piece about the Negroes he had observed in the countryside around Washington. Everywhere on his tramps he had met the "freedmen" trudging along the road or in the fields and woods, sometimes accompanied by a tame opossum on its owner's shoulders or by a fox on a leash. As might be expected, Burroughs' main interest, whether he is discussing a southern Negro or an Englishman, is in a human being's relationship to the soil, to the climate, and to the resources of his environment. The Negro, he finds, is an expert hunter and trapper; but, above all, he is a "rude, unsophisticated peasant" (14) with precisely the same strengths all peasants possess—indeed, he has much greater strength than the poor whites who inhabit the same countryside. "There is often a benignity and depth of human expression and sympathy about some of the dark faces that comes [*sic*] home to one like the best one sees in art or reads in books" (14). He compares them to "the simple English stock" (14) from which his own grandparents sprang; in fact, he sees himself in them and believes they see themselves in him—and adds that "neither party has much to boast of" (14). He attributes to the Negro of his day about the same degree of development as characterized the Anglo-Saxon countrymen of fifty or sixty years earlier, for the Negroes have the same superstitions, fears of ghosts, and the like, and practice a "shouting" Methodism now virtually extinct among the whites. Admiring the abilities and ingenuities of the white man—especially of the Yankees—the Negro is still content to occupy a subordinate position but is nevertheless making noticeable progress in mastering white people's ways. Doubtless by present-day standards, Burroughs would be considered condescending toward the black man. His presentation of him as a picturesque feature of the landscape is perhaps a bit in the manner of southern writers from John Pendleton Kennedy to William Faulkner. But Burroughs' attitude is certainly less condescending than that of most writers of his day who claimed to be well-disposed toward the Negro—Whitman, for example.

    Winter Sunshine also received favorable reviews, and among the most favorable was one by Henry James, Jr., in *The Nation* (January 27, 1876). "This is a charming little book," wrote James, who had already read parts of it as periodical articles. He found the essays "slender and light, but . . . [with] a real savour of their own. . . . The minuteness of [Burroughs'] observation, the keenness of his perception . . . give him a real originality, which is confirmed by a style sometimes indeed idiomatic and unfinished to a fault, but capable of remarkable felicity and vividness."[6] Making the inevitable comparison, James describes Burroughs as "a sort of reduced, but also more humorous, more available, and more sociable Thoreau." He thinks that the essay on England, "An October Abroad," "really deserves to become classical" because of its winning combination of freshness and naïvité.

III *Man in Nature*

    A reason for Burroughs' success with readers of his outdoor essays is that he never totally excludes himself from whatever phase of nature he is describing. Invariably, he is present, at least as an offstage commentator, but usually as a participant. Frequently there are other actors as well. Thus, in *Locusts and Wild Honey* (1879), several essays—such as "Speckled Trout," and "A Bed of Boughs"—contain, among other matter, first-person narrative accounts of trout-fishing expeditions made by Burroughs and one or more companions. Comparison may be made with Ernest Hemingway's trout-fishing stories and with chapters in his novels, but the award for better writing is by no means automatically his. The love that both authors have for the sport underlies their writing about it, as does also their even greater love of the clear, cold streams and the forests where the fishing takes place. The personal feelings of each are revealed indirectly but surely and become the chief delight of their accounts of the companionship, the simple living, and the plain and heartening food and drink that characterize such outings. Burroughs and his companions live almost entirely on the fish they catch and on the milk and bread purchased at remote farmhouses they chance to be near—the equivalent of the *vin du pays* drunk by Hemingway's fishermen. Both authors write not only about their fishing but about the people they meet—farmers, peasants, woodsmen, boys. Both are scrupulously undidactic, of course. The fishing is an end in itself, almost a ritual.

These fishing essays contained the best writing that Burroughs had thus far done, but others of equal merit followed. Most of his outstanding nature essays continued, however, to describe not just nature alone but people doing things in nature. Frequently, too, there is an added motif—that of availing oneself of nature's bounty. This concept is definitely present in the fishing pieces, in which the sportsmen live off their catches. Another fine example is "An Idyll of the Honey Bee," in *Pepacton* (1881). Quite aside from its literary charm, which is great, this essay is a fascinating, instructive account of a backwoods calling long extinct—that of the bee-hunter. Burroughs himself had become expert in bee-hunting as a way of availing himself of one of nature's gifts, and he had become acquainted with the habits of the bee, which he describes in this essay. But he does much more; he also describes in great detail the hunter at work.

A comparison with James Fenimore Cooper's treatment of the same subject enhances one's appreciation of Burroughs' essay. Readers of *The Prairie* are introduced to Paul Hover, a bee-hunter, whose speech is composed largely of metaphors taken from his occupation. Granting that Paul Hover represents a type to be found on the frontier, the reader is left with no understanding of what his work really is like, and Paul Hover—even his tag name is a hindrance to bringing him to life—never seems other than a thing of cardboard. A man's character is in part formed by his work, and all the better novelists have known this; and most of them have also known—though Henry James seems to be an exception—that a man who does no work is likely to be deficient in character. Burroughs, though he seldom intentionally composes a character sketch, does in this essay write about himself as a bee-hunter and thus provides the reader with a satisfying spectacle of an individual pursuing a calling with skill and pertinacity and with the quiet courage that all good work requires.

IV   *The Nature Writer's Diary*

For Burroughs, the stance of the purely objective scientist was impossible and repugnant. He went into the fields and woods to observe living birds and animals and to present them as lifelike as possible in his essays. In *Indoor Studies* he wrote: "my interest in nature is not strictly a scientific one. I seldom, for instance, go into a natural history museum without feeling as if I were attending a funeral" (49)—which is to say that to him science seemed more closely related to death than to life. And in the prefatory note in *Riverby* (1894) he described himself as "an interested spectator of the *life* [emphasis added] of nature, as, with the changing seasons, it has ebbed and flowed past my door." At the time he was preparing *Riverby* for the press, Burroughs thought it would be his last volume of outdoor pieces (actually four or five more followed), and he speculates from time to time about the characteristics of such writing as he has practiced it. Continuously, for instance, he repeats that nature must be studied out-of-doors, not in textbooks and laboratories, where it becomes lifeless and meaningless. One must approach nature with feminine intuition and sensitivity. Invaluable to the nature lover is a diary, Burroughs writes in "Spring Jottings," for one does not truly *live* his experiences until he transmits them through the point of a pen. The act of writing brings to the conscious level impressions that otherwise would remain unconscious, as an angler with his hook and line brings up the unseen fish from far beneath the surface. And, once captured in a journal, the best and most profound moments of living are always available for renewal.

In giving extracts from his own journal, he illustrates the process not only of fishing impressions from the unconscious but of transforming them into pure poetry. The following excerpt crescendoes into a highly poetic utterance: "The top of a high barometric wave, a day like a crest, lifted up, sightly, sparkling. A cold snap without storm issuing in this clear, dazzling, sharp, northern sky. How light, as if illuminated by more than the sun; the sky is full of light; light seems to be streaming up all around the horizon. The leafless trees make no shadows; the woods aie flooded with light; everything shines; a day large and imposing, breathing strong masculine breaths out of the north; a day without a speck or a film, winnowed through and through, all the windows and doors of the sky open. Day of crumpled rivers and lakes, of crested waves, of bellying sails, high-domed and lustrous day." And then in the final sentence, one has the inevitable lapse back into the prosaic: "The only typical March day of the bright heroic sort we have yet had" (173-74).

Impressions, whether "poetical" or not, form in the unconscious mind and issue forth in the quiet retrospection of diary writing, later to be used at the author's discretion in his writing for publication. A Freudian would surely agree that at least some of the diary entries are the true stuff of the unconscious, for frequently the language is bluntly sexual, and this may be retained in the finished essays. Thus, in "Spring Jottings" the entry for April 12, 1890, reads: "How I delight to see the plough at work such mornings! the earth is ripe for it, fairly lusts for it . . ." (180).

V   *Sharp Eyes*

Throughout his writing Burroughs stresses the importance of close observation, which is needed as much in the study of literature and of the abstract sciences as in the study of nature in the field. *Signs and Seasons* (1886), a volume of outdoors pieces, begins appropriately enough with an essay entitled "A Sharp Lookout," describing the rewards of careful watching. For the accurate watcher, nature unrolls a spectacle of infinite variety, interest, and significance. But Burroughs is not presenting a set of instructions for field naturalists—a technique for the discovery of new facts about the world around us. To Burroughs, being a successful naturalist constitutes being at home in nature— attuning oneself to her and becoming merged in her: "One's own landscape comes in time to be a sort of outlying part of himself; he has sowed himself broadcast upon it, and it reflects his own moods and feelings . . ." (5).

Knowledge of nature becomes knowledge of self. Scientific fact is all very well, but its true significance lies in what it contributes to self-knowledge. The poet's or essayist's function is to make such significance apparent, and Burroughs considers himself from this standpoint as much a poet as a scientist. A science concerned solely with facts was repugnant to him, and even more repugnant is the man described in "Bird Enemies" who "collects" eggs for no reason other than proving his prowess in hunting down his plunder. Such persons are on a level with the gatherers of milliners' plumage—destroyers rather than observers and lovers of nature's beauty. The real ornithologist will take a bird's life only as a last resort in establishing truth—a modification of Burroughs' earlier view that a gun was an indispensable piece of the ornithologist's equipment.

In addition to glimpses of her beauties, nature grants the conscientious observer philosophic, perhaps religious, insights. For example, a study of the way trees send out tentative roots in search of water illustrates the blind, groping, untiring impulse of nature in the myriad forms of life that appear and disappear upon the planet—the impulse which constitutes the one certainty and the deepest riddle in man's terrestrial existence. Or, in a snowstorm, which Burroughs describes in a ten-page prose lyric that should be compared with Emerson's famous poem on the subject, "we are admitted to Nature's oldest laboratory, and see the working of the law by which the foundations of the material universe were laid,—the law or mystery of crystallization" (102-3). Or, again, at the shore of the ocean one is brought face to face with still another of the great mysteries, that of the origin of all life—an experience recorded in Whitman's "Out of the Cradle Endlessly Rocking," which Burroughs adduces in the essay "A Salt Breeze" as an example of the religious emotions that can be generated by close and sympathetic contact with nature.

Thus, meaningful observation of nature is a search for spiritual values—for that which gives delight to the mind and a glow to the soul. Thoreau's observation in *Walden* is of this type, but in his diaries it is mostly of the forms of nature—mere scrutiny of surfaces—and hence of little interest to Burroughs. For all his incessant spying on nature, Thoreau, in Burroughs' opinion, made precious few real observations (as opposed to scrutiny)—an accusation which is also leveled against Richard Jefferies. Whitman, of course, is preeminent among the true observers. "In literature," Burroughs would say, "never Nature for her own sake, but for the sake of the soul which is over and above all" (*Riverby*, 232). In sum, effective observation involves total engagement. One must be in tune mentally and spiritually with the object of one's search.

VI   *Nature Fakers*

In the *Atlantic Monthly* of March, 1903, was printed an article by Burroughs, "Real and Sham Natural History," which began a controversy that lasted for years and released an avalanche of rebuttals and confirmations. An outgrowth of his own devotion to accurate perception, the essay was surprisingly hostile for the mild-tempered Burroughs. The target of the attack was that class of nature writing in which birds and animals are humanized to an extent totally unsupportable by science or objective investigation. Burroughs was not opposed to writing that was frankly fanciful in its presentation of animals, but he vehemently deplored fantasy that claimed to be scientifically true. After listing a number of authors—such as Bradford Torrey and Dallas L. Sharp—who do not offend, he assails two very popular ones, Ernest Thompson Seton and the Reverend William Long, who do offend. He handles Seton less roughly than he does Long, though he suggests that Seton's *Wild Animals I have Known* might more appropriately have been named *Wild Animals I Alone Have Known*.

As for Long, Burroughs exerts no restraint in ridiculing his *School in the Woods,* which contends, among other absurdities, that the birds methodically train their young in schools resembling human classrooms—even, Burroughs sarcastically suggests, to the point of having examining boards and issuing diplomas. Most reprehensible about Long is that he offers these fantasies as proved facts. His deception is intentional and more brazen than that of other writers, many of whom are mawkishly sentimental rather than consciously mendacious. But whatever their motives, many nature writers were foisting nonsense upon an all-too-gullible public: tales of foxes that ride on sheep's backs to elude pursuit, or lead a hound to his death on a railroad trestle just as a train thunders onto it, as if the fox carried a timetable with him; yarns of beasts committing suicide or poisoning their young to save them from captivity; and stories of birds setting their broken legs in casts of mud.

Burroughs' well-deserved attack was long overdue. Immediately letters of congratulation from other naturalists poured in—among them one from Theodore Roosevelt, then president of the United States, who detested what he called the "nature fakers." The correspondence with Roosevelt on the subject, some of which Burroughs quoted in later essays, continued for several years, the two being in agreement except on minor points. Roosevelt was particularly incensed that schoolchildren should be taught falsehoods—counteracting the truthful accounts of animals in those essays of Burroughs that were being used as reading texts. As the president did not wish publicly to enter the lists, he contented himself with encouraging those whose point of view he shared. Finally, however, his restraint deserted him and in June, 1907, he allowed *Everybody's Magazine* to publish an interview with him in which he vehemently vented his opinion. Shortly thereafter a panel of professional naturalists gave Roosevelt and Burroughs their support in the same periodical. Under these crushing attacks the opposition was quieted, and the controversy ended. Allied with the president and, doubtlessly, with the truth, Burroughs had carried his point. The public was made well aware of where error lay, and editors, who had come in for their share of chiding, would for a time be more circumspect.

In a letter written to a friend at this time, Burroughs expressed wonder that Roosevelt, with all his fights in Washington, should be able to find time and energy for this relatively insignificant quarrel. But perhaps it was not so insignificant to the president, who had come under attack for killing animals needlessly on his widely publicized hunting expeditions. His political enemies would stand to gain if he could be made to appear insensitive to the suffering of wild creatures and the more nearly human these could be made to appear the more heartless would the president seem. Citizens fed with the mawkish stuff of many of the nature writers might even be influenced in their voting. The article by Burroughs—an honored naturalist and a household name to the generations brought up on his essays in the schools—could have appeared something of a godsend. This is not to say that Roosevelt, who was an extremely able field naturalist himself, had no regard for the truth; he was doubtlessly genuinely pained by some of the prevarications that so-called nature writers got into print.

Nor is there any reason to think that Roosevelt did not have a genuine affection and admiration for "Oom [uncle] John," as he affectionately called Burroughs. He had already corresponded with Burroughs as early as 1893, expressing his agreement with the ideas in the essays "Before Genius" and "Before Beauty." Now after the nature-faker controversy erupted, a close friendship developed between the two—but still with political dividends to Roosevelt. In 1903 Roosevelt took Burroughs with him on a trip to Yellowstone National Park. As the train crossed the continent, Burroughs seemed almost to rival the president in the esteem of the crowds that had gathered. As for Roosevelt, whose reputation as a ferocious hunter might make people suspicious as to what his purpose was in going to Yellowstone, what better company could he be seen in than that of the benign and bearded Seer of Slabsides? Burroughs was enough the shrewd Catskill farmer to suspect some such motivation on his great friend's part; and years later, after a visit with him at Pine Knot, Virginia, Burroughs delayed until after Roosevelt's death the printing of an article describing the visit although Roosevelt had quite openly urged its earlier publication.

Yet the two were often together at the White House, at Oyster Bay, and once at Slabsides; and in his *Camping with President Roosevelt* (1906), Burroughs wrote glowingly of his great friend. He admired him as an outdoorsman and as a statesman, and he thought of him as fulfilling Whitman's specifications for the new type of democratic manhood that would arise in the United States. Only years later, when Roosevelt was sniping at Woodrow Wilson, whom Burroughs deeply respected, did Burroughs' admiration diminish, and then only slightly. Passive and unaggressive to a fault, Burroughs was somewhat awestruck by this man who could hunt lions and tigers, put at bay the rapacious trusts, induce warring nations to lay down their arms, and send a fleet around the globe to demonstrate America's might.

The importance of the victory in the nature-faker controversy should not be overlooked among these more portentous considerations. Much of American literature, from its beginnings, has been concerned with nature in her various aspects, and certainly the nature essay as written by Audubon, Thoreau, Burroughs, and many others has been one of the major national literary achievements. Gladly leaving a place for self-announced fiction or fantasy, Burroughs merely insisted that in nonfiction the truth should be approximated.

VII   *Truthful Nature Writing*

The standards of truthfulness that Burroughs established for nature writing appear in the essays in *Ways of Nature* (1905). To begin with, Burroughs himself conceded that animals share the human faculties of "perception, sense memory, and association of memories . . ." (vi). He also recognizes in animals such basic emotions as fear, jealousy, maternal love, and sexual love. Of reason or of morality he grants them nothing, or extremely little. What appears to be reason is usually instinct, which he defines as inborn, unlearned modes of behavior in given circumstances—"a kind of natural reason . . . that acts without proof or experience" (76-77). To new circumstances outside the experience and the memory of a species, the birds and beasts show little ability to adjust; for example, the birds will fight with their own image in a pane of glass for hours or until total exhaustion overcomes them.

Those nature writers that endow birds and animals with "almost the entire human psychology" are simply "romancers" (13), who either deliberately lie or cannot use their eyes. One result of this portrayal is a maudlin sentimentality that expresses itself in the founding of hospitals for sick cats and in fanatic condemnation of vivisection.

By setting a limit to animal powers, Burroughs does not intend to demean them. Their instincts can accomplish some remarkable feats, as is the case with the homing instinct, which he describes in a once popular essay, "The Wit of a Duck"—the story of a drake who finds his way home after being taken several miles away in a bag from which he could see nothing. Indeed, instinct places animals above man in some ways, and he has had to learn laboriously the skills he needs for survival. His humbler fellow creatures are born with their skills already perfected—the ability to swim, to fly, to build nests; but these accomplishments must be differentiated from the achievements of a reasoning intelligence.

Similar caution is needed in gauging the animals' powers of communication among themselves. Some communication, of course, does exist, even between species. Fear, for example, is eminently transferable by vocal sounds and by contagion. Other emotions also can be communicated. But "communication of knowledge" (87-88), conscious teaching, Burroughs rules out. Animals do not teach, even by example; but they can in certain situations, like that of danger, impart their emotions to their young so that the result looks like conscious instruction. For example, in the presence of a trap, a fox feels fear, which is transferred to the young, who henceforth associate traps with fear. But the mother fox does not in any manner reason with her young about the danger of traps in general.

To Burroughs, the most mysterious type of animal communication is that which activates herds of quadrupeds, flocks of birds, and schools of fish. The faculty is truly marvelous, and beyond human comprehension, that enables five hundred grackles, for instance, to wheel about in the air, reverse directions, alight on a tree or field, and take off again, all as a single organism, with a precision of movement not remotely approached by the best trained army or ballet corps. What lies behind such spectacles of motion en masse? Burroughs speculates that it may be a power of mental telepathy analogous to that which underlies mob movements but stronger and more dependable. Truly this mass-mindedness is one of the wonders of nature, far more impressive than the imperfect approximations to human reason credited to animals by the nature fakers.

As for the claims made by the nature fakers that animal behavior varies in different places and in different individuals, Burroughs echoes Thoreau in replying that "what one observes truly ... on his farm of ten acres, he will not have to unlearn, travel wide or as far as he will" (101-2). Burroughs is a total mechanist so far as birds and beasts are concerned, for he sees their lives as governed from birth to death by outer forces and by inner, unreasoning instinct. Moreover, "instinct is not always inerrant" (111), but develops in animals by the usual wasteful evolutionary trial-and-error process. The law of variation, especially among solitary animals, always obtains; but the variations are slight, never so extensive as among human beings. "Nature learns by endless experiment" (139), but it is nature, the "cosmic intelligence" (129), that is doing the learning for the animals and controlling them.

All animals of the same species behave very nearly the same everywhere. The difficulty in noting variations lies in the scarcity of investigators who do not permit their own emotions or predilections to color the truth or to blind them to part of it. Not that Burroughs would exclude personal feeling from man's enjoyment of nature—only from his professedly objective observation of her. In a fine essay, "Bird Songs" in *Ways of Nature*, he readily admits now much temperament, memories, the past enter into the songs one hears. "Bird-songs are not music, properly speaking, but only suggestions of music. ... Their merit as musical performances is very slight" (29-31). Hence a song of a caged bird removed from the beauties of meadows and woods is usually a disappointment. But, for example, the flight song of the woodcock (which Burroughs heard only three times in his life) is sheer rhapsody when one hears it at dusk in a lonely pasture in the company of a good companion.

Burroughs' description of this experience in the essay "Straight Seeing and Thinking" (*Leaf and Tendril*, 119ff.), is one of the most lyrical passages in all his writings and is freighted with personal feeling. However, Burroughs realizes that the flight song of the woodcock, as well as the flight songs of other birds, are expressions of sheer ecstasy on the part of the singer; for joy is one of the emotions animals share with man. Yet the listener's own feelings, he insists, supply most of the music and poetry he hears, though one need not be a poet to effect the transformation. Burroughs tells of an old Irishman, who on hearing a lark singing above him took off his hat and stood transported, with tears on his cheeks. He was not only hearing the bird but was reliving his lost youth in the old country, of which the bird reminded him.

VIII   *What it Is to Be Human*

Burroughs' consideration of animal intelligence leads him into a subject of greater importance both to him and to his reader—what it is to be a human being, or what the essential differences are that set man off from other forms of life. A major one is that animals are unable to profit from their experiences by generalizing upon them, as can man. They are capable of perception but not conception (*Ways of Nature*, 140), for conception-making ability is uniquely human. Thus a whole gamut of emotions that arise from concepts are denied to animals. For instance, guilt arises from a sense of justice—which is an abstraction or concept. Burroughs denies that the dog that has done wrong and grovels before his master feels guilt. He fears his masters' anger rather than remorse for a misdeed, which he will repeat unless chastised. Not even the most inveterate dog lovers, of which Burroughs is one, seriously appeals to his pet's conscience. Similarly, feelings arising from concepts of "truth, beauty, altruism, goodness, duty" (143) are foreign to the lower animals, which, he repeats time and again, are machines acted upon by universal forces beyond their comprehension or control. Man, though he too is in the clutches of his racial heritage and his environment, has some area for free choice and action based on conceptual thinking and on abstractions denied the animals.

Through all of organic and inorganic nature Burroughs, as will be seen in more detail later, postulates a cosmic soul manifesting itself in varying forms and with differing degrees of flexibility. Nature's "thinking is more flexible and adaptive in the vegetable than in the mineral, and more so in the animal than in the vegetable, and most of all in the mind of man" (152-53); but Burroughs emphasizes that human intelligence differs from that of animals in "kind and not merely [in] degree" (229). Man, indeed, seems partway along the road to self-determination—the halfway condition in which Dreiser in *Sister Carrie* sees the race. Man thus lives not only on the "plane of sense" along with animals but, uniquely, on a "plane of spirit" (161). In man, the cosmic soul—the equivalent of Emerson's oversoul—has its most significant, because most creative, expression. An animal is born with the instinctive capability of performing certain acts—suckling its mother, fleeing danger, flying or walking or running—but it cannot cope with combinations of circumstances hitherto entirely unknown to it or to the ancestors from which it derived its instincts. Any accounts of animals meeting a new set of conditions with imagination and reasoning should be taken with "a pinch of salt" (the title of one of Burroughs' essays on the subject). "Because man . . . is half animal, shall we say that the animal is half man?" (170) Burroughs' answer is a resounding *No*.

IX *The Role of the Nature Writer*

What then about the nature writer? What is his function? In an essay "The Literary Treatment of Nature" Burroughs gives his answers. There is a legitimate and very useful activity for the belletrist who wishes to make nature his subject, but his role is definitely not the purveying of untruths unless labeled as such, that is, as romantic fantasy. The function that Burroughs approves is the one he attempts to perform—that of the nature essayist, who must be carefully differentiated from the scientific naturalist. The latter gathers and records facts; his appeal is limited largely to other scientists. The former—the nature essayist—also bases his works on facts, which he gathers in the field with the greatest care. But, as an essayist, he rearranges, synthesizes, and generalizes his findings so as to appeal to feelings, arouse interest, and give a feeling of rapport with nature. He attempts to show living nature in its totality—the whole bird in the tree or the forest, as opposed to, say, a microscopically analyzed cross section of its tail feathers.

The nature essayist must attempt to induce in his readers the experience of self-revelation. One sees himself in the animals when he sees them without mawkishness—or he sees that part of himself which consists of instinct, racial memories and impulses, and the will to struggle with environment. Burroughs is not backing away from his former position, for he is not suddenly recommending that man anthropomorphize the animals. When, for example, Thoreau describes the battle of the ants, he in no way falsifies the facts. What interests or fascinates one in the ants, as Thoreau describes them, is the "human traits of courage, fortitude, heroism, self-sacrifice" (195) that they exhibit. Men, too, become involved in battles in which the same traits are important in deciding the issue. There is no question of attributing uniquely human traits, like reason or language communication, to the ants. Indeed, if an author made such attributions, he would lessen the interest and value of his account by rendering it harder to believe.

But the ants in their battles actually do display hardihood, stubbornness, selflessness; these are observable facts. These glimpses of animal behavior are important to man because in them he perceives his own kinship with all organic matter; he understands his share in the evolutionary past from which he sprang. To this extent—the extent of the truth—the animals may be humanized, but no further. And this the best literary presentations of animals do: Burns's mouse, Maeterlinck's bees, John Muir's dog Stickeen. And today one might add others: Steinbeck's turtle and red pony, Van Tilburg Clark's panther, Hemingway's marlin, Faulkner's bear and various dogs—for American literature is rich in animal representations, and the best meet the specifications that Burroughs outlined. Doubtlessly the standards he established and which came to be editorially accepted did much, however indirectly, to improve American nature writing.

Stories or essays which present animals as they really are awake genuine emotions and feelings of kinship without straining the reader's willingness to believe; however, the author must first have these feelings himself before he can hope to kindle them in the reader. Ultimately, then, the nature writer does what all creative writers must do: he communicates his own experiences. In this way he differs, on the one hand, from the scientific naturalist, whose purpose is to supply facts alone and, on the other hand, from the fabulist, whose use of animals is to teach moral lessons. Both of these are worthwhile functions, but they should not be confused with the primarily esthetic appeal of the nature essayist or the realistic fiction writer. The scientist describes the animal, the fabulist uses it to teach a lesson, but the belleletrist should strive to make one love or admire it for what it is.

X   Travel to England

Akin to his nature writing are Burroughs' accounts of his travels. While still working for the United States Treasury in 1871, Burroughs was one of three employees sent to England to deliver $15,000,000 in government bonds. Since his official duties required little time, he had the month of October for travel. The result—the last one hundred pages of *Winter Sunshine*, entitled "An October Abroad"—was the first and some of the best of his travel writing, which forms a rather impressive segment of his work. These early essays, like his later ones, are more than mere travel descriptions: they are personal essays in the strictest sense of the term. "I will say at the outset," Burroughs writes, "that in this narrative I shall probably describe myself more than the objects I look upon" (145). And in the preface to the book he states that "the sensations of the first day are what we want,—the first flush of the traveler's thought and feeling . . ." (v). Henry James, as has been seen, agreed that such an objective was a good one for writing travel literature.

With frankly avowed subjectivity, Burroughs was doing in his travel essays precisely what he had advocated doing in nature essays; and the distinction between the two genres, as Burroughs writes them, is not very great. But he was doing in addition what a long line of earlier American travel writers had done—among them Irving, Cooper, Longfellow, Hawthorne, Emerson, and Melville—when they gave way to their emotions at first sight of the places of their origins. Burroughs, like many of his predecessors, writes mainly about England because his feelings are most deeply involved with it through his ancestry, language, and "inheritance of English ideas and predilections," so that "much of what he sees affects him like a memory" (vi). Of Ireland and France, which he visited briefly, he speaks with a scorn born of Anglo-Saxon prejudice.

The highly domesticated, parklike English landscape, which contrasted so strongly with the shaggier, rougher terrain of his native Catskills, caused pleasant astonishment. In England, he thought, the land had been so long lived on, so long cultivated and molded to human needs, not only for sustenance but for beauty, that it contained no more wilderness than a carefully tended garden—but the garden seemed almost deserted owing to the English farmers' living in the villages, after the medieval custom, and coming forth whenever agricultural tasks required. Burroughs was also struck by the air of permanence—absent in America—of the English scene as typified by the ancient stone, arched bridges everywhere in evidence, even spanning the smallest creeks on the farms. Indeed, these arched bridges were to Burroughs perfect expressions of the solidity of the British character.

The unfamiliar birds of the island, of course, intrigued Burroughs immensely, but one need not linger over his ornithological comments, for his comments about London are of wider interest. The British metropolis, he finds, has less splendor than New York but a closer affinity with the countryside, as is indicated by place names in the city—roads instead of avenues, for example—and by the numerous completely rustic parks which are a marvel of delight to him. As for architecture, he soon realized that he had never before seen "a building with genius and power in it, and that one could look at with the eye of the imagination" (171). He was overwhelmed by St. Paul's.

As for the masses of the people, he considered the London crowd "the most normal and unsophisticated [he] had ever seen, with the least admixture of rowdyism and ruffianism" (196)—a welcome contrast with the "brazen ruffianism in our great cities" (195). "England is a mellow country, and the English people are a mellow people" (186), Burroughs writes. The country is mellowed not only by its long history of human cultivation but also and more basically by its climate. Always something of a determinist—a seeker of scientific reasons to explain why things are as they are—Burroughs devotes pages to the effects of climate on all phases of English life. Because of the moderateness of the weather, the old stone buildings last longer, woolen clothes are worn the year around, one may exercise out-of-doors in all seasons, the landscape is greener. Climate has no less an effect on the physical appearance of the English, whose features are coarser—less sharpened and refined than those of the Americans, whose complexions are ruddier, and whose voices are softer.

Lapsing, as Burroughs frequently did in the 1870s into the archaic medical vocabulary gained in the days he was reading to be a physician, he attributes to weather the fundamental differences of character and temperament between the English and Americans: "Our climate is more heady and less stomachic than the English; sharpens the wit, but dries up the fluids and viscera; favors an irregular, nervous energy, but exhausts the animal spirits" (163). The American's energies "are constantly leaving his stomach in the lurch, and running off into his hands and feet and head. . . . We have not enough constitutional inertia and stolidity; our climate gives us no rest, but goads us day and night. . . We are playing the game more rapidly, and I fear less thoroughly and sincerely, than the mother country" (164).

Such meteorological determinism of national character accounts for many but not all of the differences between the English and the Americans. Other differences, Burroughs points out, are the result of a unique and longer British history and of a distinctive racial composition. But, whatever the causes, Burroughs is so impressed by things English that he finds it necessary to protest that he does not find *everything* superior in England—only, one might add, almost everything. He sees America in the process of catching up with the British culture from which she sprang and eventually outstripping it; he accepts Whitman's concept of America as a young giant who, while profiting from the best in the heritage from the past, will leave that past far behind in an advance toward a perfect society. If there have been some detours in the forward movement, as even Whitman admitted there had been, the promise is so great and so certain that any look backward to the starting point in the Old World is time wasted. But Burroughs constantly looked back, especially through the windows of English literature; and what he saw in England filled him with a nostalgia and a somewhat sentimental admiration that were enhanced by the many crudities in his own country. Although at only one period in his life, at the time of Harding's election to the presidency and the United States' repudiation of the League of Nations, did Burroughs say he was ashamed of being an American, he was never the highly vocal or deeply convinced patriot that his two friends Whitman and Theodore Roosevelt were.

Nine years later Burroughs included in *Fresh Fields* (1884) several essays based on his second trip in 1882 to England and Scotland. He elaborates on his earlier ideas but introduces few new ones. There is much on British birds and flora as contrasted with American ones, and there is a lengthy account of a quest, mainly abortive, to hear the nightingale's song. The remainder of the volume consists of essays about Wordsworth and Carlyle, the latter of which have been discussed elsewhere.

XI   *The Harriman Expedition*

A third volume devoted largely to travel accounts is *Far and Near* (1904), which begins with a 129-page description of a journey to Alaska and ends with a 54-page piece, "A Lost February," about a visit to Jamaica. In 1899 E. H. Harriman, the railroad tycoon, invited Burroughs to join an expedition of exploration to Alaska. Since the group was not to be a bushwhacking or dog-sledding one, the members included the Harriman family (Averell, a little boy, went along) and various experts, among them John Muir, a student of glaciers; B. E. Fernow, a dendrologist; G. B. Grinnell, an ethnologist; and R. Swain Gifford, a landscape painter. Burroughs, the historian of the expedition, was to write the general narrative account that would comprise the first part of a multivolumed record. (This narrative, somewhat altered, is reprinted in *Far and Near*.) The group was to cross the continent by private train, stop at points of interest along the way, and then proceed by chartered ship along the coast to Bering Straits.

Burroughs accepted Harriman's invitation with some reluctance, for he questioned whether the expedition would afford opportunity for fruitful investigation and disliked the idea of being assigned a writing task. His custom was to go to nature and later to write about her, but only if so moved, never from a feeling of compulsion. Furthermore, he feared that the luxury in which they would travel and the numbers of people would make impossible any important scientific work. But, so far as his own writing goes, Burroughs need not have worried: his account of the journey contains some of his most vivid and interesting pages—informal, varied in subject matter, lively throughout, and occasionally humorous.

Both the journeys described in *Far and Near*—the one to Alaska and the other to Jamaica—did more for Burroughs than provide him with material for a book. Although he was sixty-two when he went to Alaska, he had never been west of the Mississippi nor south of the temperate zone. John Muir frequently rallied Burroughs about the narrowness of his acquaintance with nature. Indeed, except for the desolation of the ocean that Burroughs had experienced on his European voyages, he had known nature only in rather benign aspects: the rounded, wooded slopes of the northern Appalachians; the orchards and pastures of New York and New England; the even tamer countryside along the Potomac; the sandy, surf-laced Atlantic seaboard; and the gardenlike landscape of the British Isles.

Burroughs had seen, in short, much beauty and some grandeur, as in his own Hudson Valley; but he was almost totally inexperienced in scenery that inspires awe, terror, revulsion, or a sense of nature's indifference, if not hostility, to man. His concept of the wild was similar to Thoreau's—a rather benign and wholesome influence that can be enjoyed in the genial environs of Concord or the Catskills with occasional excursions to the seashore and the north woods. One wonders what modification Thoreau's outlook would have undergone had he ever traveled outside the northeastern quadrant of the United States and adjacent areas in Canada. Good as it was to travel far in Concord, or in Ulster County, New York, other vistas might have added new dimensions to Thoreau's philosophy, as they did to Burroughs'. For after his trips to Alaska and to Jamaica, Burroughs was never again wholly at ease in nature's lap—never quite so certain that all that is natural is generally for the best. His first volume after the Alaskan trip, *The Light of Day* (1900), questions the ways of nature and betrays an awareness of the "cosmic chill," as he called the terrifying aspect of the universe, that increased during the rest of his life.

Soon after Mr. Harriman's private train had crossed the Mississippi, Burroughs sustained some shocks. The treeless monotony of the Great

Plains, the appalling meanness and poverty of the farms in the mountain states, the nightmarishness of the Badlands, all gave assurance of an unfriendly side of nature. There were also splendors and fertility—for example, the Multnomah Falls in Oregon; the Laramie Plain, green in late May and covered with grazing cattle; and the gentle, feminine hills along the Snake River, which he compared to the South Downs of England. Indeed, included in these descriptions are traces of the old American dream and myth of a New World Eden, with a new chance for a new man. But Burroughs' overall feeling about the great West was an uncomfortable astonishment, almost a sense of betrayal, at the discovery that such expanses could be so forbidding, so different from the friendly glade at Slabsides or the home meadows in Roxbury.

The shocks continued as the party boarded ship and steamed northward. Burroughs viewed lovely sunsets, the stupendous beauty of the Fayerweather Range; the loveliness of the beflowered arctic tundra; and, above all, the soft charms of Kodiak, where the Old Russian village nestled on the green and rolling landscape and the people followed the normal, wholesome activities of fishermen and farmers. Kodiak, which reminded him of home, inspired him to write several poems, the first he had attempted in a long time and ones better than his distressingly mediocre average. But there was a painful opposite effect. The spectacle at White Pass actually frightened him: "It was as appalling to look up as to look down; chaos and death below us, impending avalanches of hanging rocks above us. How elemental and cataclysmal it all looked! I felt as if I were seeing for the first time the real granite ribs of the earth. ... All I had seen before were but scabs and warts on the surface by comparison; here were the primal rocks that held the planet together, sweeping up into the clouds and plunging down into the abyss" (37). The Muir Glacier, despite its grandeur, filled him with an only slightly less uncomfortable awe.

XII   *A Glimpse of the Tropics and Travels with Muir*

The impressions of Jamaica, which Burroughs and his son Julian visited in 1902, as described in "A Lost February," were somewhat less mixed than those of Alaska. Nature in the tropics seemed entirely unlovable to Burroughs and not conducive to the friendly relationship he was accustomed to enjoy with her. Instead of open forests that invited one for a stroll, there were impenetrable jungles. Everything was spiked and fanged—cacti and reptiles seemed to dominate this land "cursed with perpetual summer" (223). The native inhabitants were lazy and ambitionless—a disturbingly standard reaction for a white traveler in a black country. In fact, in discussing the poverty and drabness of the life of the natives both in Alaska and in Jamaica, Burroughs displays little or no compassion; indeed, he appears to be less interested in them than in the local flora and fauna. Aside from a few interesting birds, plants, good roads, and some fine mountain scenery—less terrifying than that in Alaska—which Burroughs deals with very briefly, he finds nature "unregenerate" (258) in Jamaica—"hard, harsh, glittering, barbaric . . ." (262). Unlike Alaska, Jamaica inspires him to write no poetry; he questions how one *could* write poetry in the tropics.

In 1909, Burroughs traveled with John Muir in the western United States and visited Hawaii. From this trip came three essays: "The Divine Abyss" (on the Grand Canyon), "The Spell of the Yosemite," and "Holidays in Hawaii," which were published in *Time and Change* (1912). By this time he was able to take more in his stride the truly awesome spectacles in nature, partly because he had developed a keen interest in geology, which helped him objectify what previously had overwhelmed him. He could now descend into the Grand Canyon or gaze into an active volcano and intellectualize about what he saw as well as emote. Furthermore, in his philosophic thought, in which he was engaging more and more, he had become preoccupied with such matters as time in terms of geologic change and with the overall structure and meaning of the universe.

"The Divine Abyss"—the only one of these essays one needs linger over—is among the more successful attempts by many authors at a verbal description of the Grand Canyon. As always, Burroughs dwells on his personal feelings even as he presents the geologic facts. He does have some of the usual emotions that have been only too frequently felt by travelers: "It is beautiful, oh, how beautiful! but it is a beauty that awakens a feeling of solemnity and awe" (47). In a letter written on his second visit to the canyon in 1911, he does a little better: "It [the Grand Canyon] is the book [*sic*] of revelation written in red carboniferous sandstone," but he then breaks into the usual exclamations of the tourist: "Such peace, such repose, such sublimity!"[7] But when he describes the descent into the canyon he is able to avoid hyperbole and gives a more restrained, factual account.

On the Alaskan voyage and on the 1909 trip to the Grand Canyon and Yosemite, John Muir was Burroughs' companion. Since it is inevitable that the two be compared, a glance at them in each other's company tells much. There was a domineering, egocentric quality in Muir that Burroughs lacked; for Muir was more the solitary, the self-sufficient mountaineer. Accustomed to the vastnesses of the Sierra, Muir was impatient of many of Burroughs' interests, especially his attachment to the Catskills. As Muir proudly displayed the wonders of the West, as if he had a proprietorship in them, he would jeeringly inquire of Burroughs if he could produce anything comparable in Ulster County. Of the many anecdotes about the bickering between the two friends, one or two may be told for their amusement if nothing else. On arriving the first time at the Grand Canyon, Burroughs announced to Muir: "I'm sleepy—I'll have to go to bed." Muir answered, "Sleepy, Johnie! Why, lad, there'll be time enough to sleep when you get back to Slabsides, or at least in the grave."[8] Later when some female gushed, "To think of our having the Grand Canyon, and John Muir and John Burroughs thrown in!" Burroughs retorted, "I wish Muir *was* thrown in sometimes . . . when he gets between me and the canyon."[9]

In literary terms, the difference between the two Johns was vast. Burroughs was in the tradition of Gilbert White of Selborne, the quiet observer of a small and highly domesticated area. Muir was the explorer of the unknown—whole mountain ranges and remote glaciers—and belongs in the tradition of explorer writers like Sir Ernest Shackleton or Mungo Park. The difference is markedly reflected in their styles, Muir's being less polished but more poetic and more panoramic than Burroughs', which, as has been seen, is simple, direct, restrained.

But these differences in personality and literary style are trivial when compared with the two men's shared enthusiasm for all of nature and their commitment to the preservation of its beauties and resources. Along with Thoreau they were the literary and spiritual forerunners of the conservation movement that has become so major an influence in recent American life and thought. Before protective measures could be taken, the nation needed to be made aware, not only of the beauty and wonder of nature, but also of the vulnerability of such essentials as fertile soil, pure water, and clean air to the spread of our technological civilization. In this educative function the writings of John Muir and John Burroughs were seminal and indispensable.

CHAPTER 5

Philosophy

I *Basic Transcendentalism*

BURROUGHS lost his belief in orthodox Christianity before his twentieth year; for, after some youthful hopes of conversion in the strictly Calvinist sense as taught by his father's Old School Baptist Church, he abandoned organized religion. Still, he was always a religious person in all but the narrowest definition of that term. He soon discovered Emerson and adopted his philosophy-religion of Transcendentalism, to which he adhered, though with modifications, for the remaining sixty-five years of his life. One should emphasize that Burroughs was always an Emersonian; though at times, under the influence of science, he may have strayed from Transcendentalism, he always returned after accommodating to it a seemingly opposing outlook. The nonscientific thinkers and writers whom he most respected—Whitman, Carlyle, Wordsworth, and Bergson—fortified him in his Transcendentalism.

Burroughs was a late but vocal and influential advocate of that brand of idealistic philosophy that had its fullest flowering in the Concord group, and he helped perpetuate it as a living force in American thought until well into the twentieth century, perhaps even to the present day. He was able to persist in idealism because he did not succumb to its extremes as taught by Bishop Berkeley in the eighteenth century: namely, that there is no objective reality outside of thought—outside of idea. In a letter to Myron Benton in 1876, he made this very clear, when he asserted that he "never took much stock in that extreme idealistic view of nature ... by which one could get rid of one's own existence just as well as of that of objective nature," for by this theory one "is only phenomenal himself—a shadow with the rest."[1] But this statement is not a repudiation—even a passing one—of Emerson, who only toyed with the Berkeleyan hypothesis and who never fully or permanently adopted it.

The foundation assumptions of Transcendentalism can be succinctly and briefly stated, and Burroughs states them many times. The following, from *Time and Change* (1912), sufficiently puts him on record as a Transcendentalist; he writes that he is convinced "that the celestial and the terrestrial are one, that time and eternity are one, that mind and matter are one, that death and life are one, that there is and can be nothing not inherent in Nature" and that one must "no longer look for or expect a far-off, unknown God" (246-47). Monism, the immediacy of God as all-pervading spirit, infinity manifested in the finite—these are the basic tenets of Transcendentalism; and almost everything Burroughs wrote rests upon them. As to how he made these a basis of his thinking becomes clear as one explores the development of his thought in the areas of science, philosophy, and theology—his writings on which stretch through his entire literary career and amount to perhaps a third of his total output.

II   *Science*

As has been stated, science was important to Burroughs for what it could contribute toward self-knowledge; for science that devoted itself solely to the accumulation of facts seemed meaningless to him. Such science could educate the intellect but not the spirit, which to Burroughs is the more important element in man. When science was used to provide knowledge of what it is to be a man by illuminating the universe of which he is a part and which is a projection of him, such usage met with Burroughs' wholehearted approval. Thus, science could be a corrective; it could keep man from misreading nature in the way the nature fakers did and consequently from confusing him as to his particularly human place in the universe. Indeed, in his earliest published work, "Vagaries *viz.* Spiritualism," printed in the Bloomville, New York, *Mirror* in 1856, Burroughs approaches with scientific objectivity what he considers a popular delusion; and he attempts to show that such delusions cannot survive the *light of day*, a phrase which forty-four years later he used as the title of a book in which he sets about the dissipation of the irrational elements that, in his opinion, becloud the conventional religions.

The Light of Day (1900), one of Burroughs' most controversial books from the point of view of the traditionally religious, does not constitute, therefore, an abrupt departure from his previous mode of thought. Consistently throughout his life he had employed science to restrain the excesses of the emotions and the imagination without in any way denying the importance of either emotions or imagination in the human makeup. The overall thesis of *The Light of Day* is expressed in the second essay, "From the Artificial to the Natural." The older theologies, like the older medicine, were complicated, fanciful, and, above all, artificial. Science has opened the way for a "natural" religion—one free of superstitions, absurdities, and monstrosities. Burroughs, of course, is in no degree an enemy of religion or of religious sentiment in man; in fact, he regards both as of supreme significance in the human lot. But a religion that totally violates reason can but poorly serve the religious sentiment. Science and religion, he emphasizes, appeal to completely different faculties. A scientifically false or unprovable religion may serve humanity well by inculcating virtue and by satisfying the need to worship. But, as Burroughs points out in a lengthy essay, "Science and Theology," it is wrong to attempt to prove scientifically propositions that cannot by the widest stretch of the imagination be made to square with science.

He is particularly condemnatory of the Scottish theologian Henry Drummond, who attempted in *Natural Law in the Spiritual World* to bolster Calvinist theology by analogies with Darwinism. Such attempts, Burroughs thinks, are not only futile and misleading but tend to obstruct the simplifying process that religious doctrine is undergoing. If one must be a Calvinist, well and good, especially if one is both a better and a happier person for it; but one should accept his Calvinism by faith rather than on spurious scientific grounds. Science, when confronted by a religion, can judge it only by that in its teachings or its results which is acceptable to science—which certainly excludes its miraculous elements. Thus, to science, Christianity is acceptable for the moral law that it enunciates through the example of Jesus. Science can recognize that Jesus "was a soul impressed, as perhaps no other soul ever had been, with the oneness of man with God, and that the kingdom of heaven is not a *place*, but a state of mind. Hence, coming to Jesus is coming to our truer, better selves, and conforming our lives to the highest ideal" (*The Light of Day*, 23). If, to follow the teaching of Jesus, one must lean on such scientifically extraneous doctrines as that of the Trinity, one is of course free to do so; but one should not try to prove rationally the truth of the doctrine. And he should not think that Christianity, when pruned of its more unprovable elements, is necessarily inferior. The whole tendency of the age is toward such pruning, with the result that the religious *sentiment*, no longer in conflict with religion, is the better served.

Always, however, Burroughs emphasizes that science is not enough; taken alone, it leads to something like despair—to the cosmic chill. For science teaches the insignificant part played in the universe by organic matter as compared to the overwhelming pervasiveness of the inorganic. Life appears only in isolated spots and for brief periods in the eternity of the sidereal ages. But this very insignificance constitutes one of its greatest wonders—and wonder is conducive to religious feeling. "Life is like a bird of passage which alights and tarries for a time and is gone, and the places where it perched and nested and led forth its brood know it no more. Apparently it flits from world to world as the great cosmic spring comes to each, and departs as the cosmic winter comes to each. It is a visitor, a migrant, a frail, timid thing, which waits upon the seasons and flees from the coming tempests and vicissitudes" (*The Breath of Life*, 116).

At best, the physical and chemical forces of the universe are indifferent to life; and in some cases, as with glaciers and geological upheavals, they seem downright hostile. But life endures; and in its most complex form, that of man, it introduces into the insensate welter of cosmic forces the ethical and esthetic values of love, justice, beauty, and freedom of will. The marvel of life—and this science alone can make man realize—is that, small as it is, it has introduced "a new element or force or tendency into the cosmos" (128)—and the most inexplicable outcome of this new force is man's mind—which, since something cannot be made of nothing, must have had its origin in intelligence, actual or potential, already existent in the universe.

III *Darwin*

Thus, the scientific approach or frame of mind guides man away from superstition to a more solidly based attitude about life and the cosmos. Science helps man square his religious emotions with his reason and thus spares him the schizophrenia of trying to make one part of himself believe what another extremely important part would like to reject. Aside from the field ornithologists Audubon, Alexander Wilson, and Wilson Flagg and amateur naturalists like White of Selbourne, all of whom had an influence in shaping Burroughs' life goals and literary style, Darwin was the scientist most inspiring to him. Indeed, Darwin's place in the development and maturing of Burroughs' thought is comparable to that of Emerson, Carlyle, and Whitman. Evolution provided one of the chief means of bridging the gap between the emotions and intuition and the religious sentiment, on the one hand,

and reason and science, on the other; and the bridging of that gap was a lifelong concern with Burroughs. In his Notebooks for 1859 there is already evidence of a leaning toward a theory of evolution in such comments as: "From a single atom, by infinite modification, Nature builds the universe. . . ." The first printed reference to Darwin occurs in the December, 1862, *Knickerbocker* in the essay "Analogy," in which Burroughs states that "Darwin's hypothesis of the derivation of species is in keeping with the unity we every where observe" (481). Some fifteen years later in the essay "Touches of Nature" in *Birds and Poets* (1877), Burroughs leans heavily on Darwin: "Wherever Nature has commissioned one creature to prey upon another, she has preserved the balance by forewarning that other creature of what she has done. . . . Nature takes care that none of her creatures have smooth sailing . . ." (49).

But the full impact of Darwin on Burroughs apparently did not occur until the latter's forty-sixth year. In his diary for August, 1883, he writes of having finished reading *The Descent of Man*: "A model of patient, tireless, sincere inquiry; such candor, such love of truth, such keen insight into the methods of Nature, such singleness of purpose, and such nobility of mind, could not be easily matched. The book convinces like Nature herself. I have no more doubt of its main conclusions than I have of my own existence."[2] And he adds in a later entry: "Darwin's theory of the descent of man adds immensely to the mystery of Nature, and to the glory of the race."[3] It in part makes man responsible, through his struggle to survive, for his greatness, whereas the traditional view of creation makes man something like an automaton, a plaything of God. As the end product of the evolutionary process, man is one with the rest of the universe, shares a kinship with all living things, and is not something special, set apart, and therefore unrelated to nature as a whole. Though this new vision of man's place in the general order may be distressing to conventional minds, it actually inspires the profoundest religious awe in those with the sensitivity and intelligence to understand its implications. To Burroughs, at least, a sense of oneness with the universe is more conducive to religious feeling than a sense of separateness.

As has been remarked, Burroughs, in the nature-faker controversy, insisted on the differences between animals and men. He would not tolerate a blurring of the distinction. But paradoxically perhaps, he also insisted that mankind is at one with the rest of the organic and inorganic universe. Evolution made it possible to accept the paradox. Man's ultimate origins coincide with those of other life forms, and much of his development he has shared with what are now the so-called lower forms. In the essay "The Long Road" (*Time and Change*, 1912), Burroughs describes the incredibly protracted history of organic nature until its culmination in man, which marked a radically new development among living things—the appearance of reason hitherto unknown and at present possessed by no other species. In this way man is truly a being apart—but in no other way; and Burroughs quite literally regards him as the culmination of evolution: nothing "higher" can evolve. For one who had rejected all dogmatic theology, Burroughs' conception of man as the darling of creation, the end-all and be-all of the planet's history, curiously suggests the Book of Genesis. To Burroughs, though, it is obvious that man and the animals possess many traits in common; man alone enjoys the Godlike "gift of reason—a gift of which he sometimes makes use" (*Leaf and Tendril*, 125). Man has outstripped the rest of organic Nature, though he is still a part of it.

Like the Social Darwinists—such men as Herbert Spencer, William Sumner, and the early Dreiser—Burroughs is able to accept in the light of evolution much that is personally repugnant to him; for man's struggle is, after all, one of the conditions of evolutionary progress. In his own life the spirit of acquisition, the greed that he sees everywhere souring and cankering modern times is absent. As he expresses his view in his poem "Waiting," he is content to remain quiescent until his own comes to him; but he insists on its being his own and not somebody else's. Yet in the accumulation of vast fortunes by aggressive and sometimes unscrupulous men—did he have in mind his old schoolmate Jay Gould?—he saw evolution at work. Though such men make a spectacle of themselves with their furious greed, they are natural phenomena that only the evolutionary process that created them can eradicate. To Burroughs, socialism would offer no solution. Yet there was a limit beyond which Burroughs could not justify struggle in human life as an inevitable manifestation of the evolutionary process. This limit was reached in World War I when the Germans attempted to rationalize their military excesses on Darwinian grounds. Such use of evolution was to Burroughs tantamount to sacrilege.

In his later years, indeed, Burroughs challenged several major assumptions made on the basis of the evolutionary hypothesis as understood in his day. In an essay, "Life the Traveler," which appeared in *Under the Apple-Trees* (1916), he critically examines the theory of natural selection. Too often, he finds, scientists speak of natural selection as an almost conscious force that purposely develops a species after some preconceived plan. Burroughs would place the purpose, the goal, of evolution within matter—first in inorganic matter, in which inheres the potential of other and higher forms, culminating in man. Thus the man potential must have been present in matter from the beginning, and the long journey of the potential was merely *aided* by natural selection—which discarded individuals and species not helpful in the steady upward advance but which did, and does, not bear a primal causative relationship with the final product.

Using a favorite phrase, Burroughs concludes that natural selection may "account for the survival of the fittest, but not for the arrival of the fittest" (265). He points out that Darwin regarded natural selection as a "process," not as a "cause" (267); and he made no attempt to explain the primal cause that started life on its travels through matter. In its simplest form, Darwinism stands for "a miraculous beginning of life, but a natural unfolding" (271). According to Darwin, living things contain an intrinsic tendency to vary without which evolution could not, of course, occur. This variation tendency Burroughs equates with Bergson's *élan vital*. Darwin, however, recognized "no innate or necessary tendency in each being to its own advancement in the scale of organization" (273). In this respect, Burroughs thinks Darwin was definitely in the wrong and Bergson in the right. He quotes Emerson to support his stand: "No statement of the universe can have any soundness that does not admit of its ascending effort" (275).

Burroughs questions even more boldly the cardinal importance of natural selection in the evolution of species. The horse, for example, evolved over a period of three million years from the two-foot-high eohippus weighing one hundred pounds to the five-foot-high, present-day animal weighing upwards of twelve hundred pounds. The horse gained one inch in height ever forty thousand years and one pound in weight every four hundred years. Such insignificant gains, Burroughs thinks, could have aided only secondarily in the battle for survival. Some other factor—to Burroughs, the Bergsonian one—must have been at work in addition to the very modest contribution of natural selection. Again, Burroughs asks why life emerged from the sea if there were not some "primal push and aspiration" (280) in addition to the struggle for survival.

These questions are surely susceptible to various answers, but Burroughs was definitely drifting away from orthodox Darwinism, though he continued to regard Darwin as the greatest of all contributors to the science of biology. There were simply too many facts that evolution could not explain on the basis of natural selection: for instance, the continuing existence in large numbers of such almost helpless beasts as the rabbit; the death of the honeybee after it stings an enemy or the death of the drone after fertilizing the queen bee—none of which phenomena would seem explainable by natural selection alone.

As for the principle of variation, Burroughs is unconvinced by the Darwinian view about the role chance plays. Touching on the hypothesis that the eye began as a pigmented spot on the epidermis, which later developed into the marvelous organ of sight, Burroughs points out that millennia must have passed before the pigmented area could have been of any great use in the struggle for survival. To him, the eye principle must have been inherent in the organism from the beginning, and recent biological theory substantiates Burroughs.

The whole subject of "Beginnings" (303) is considered and summarized in a brief essay with that title in a group—in *Under the Apple-Trees*—under the heading "Great Questions in Little." The beginning of life is inexplicable to Burroughs, who refuses to accept the theory of chance except on the basis of "an unknown and unknowable factor" (308), which he asserts "hovers in the background of the minds of even the most rigid scientists!" (308). It was present in Darwin's thought when, contradictorily to his own previous statements, he revealed his incapability of regarding the evolutionary emergence of man as the result of chance alone. It was present in John Tyndall's mind when he spoke of "the mystery and miracle of vitality" (308); in Thomas Huxley's when he postulated consciousness as a third reality along with matter and energy; and in Ernst Heinrich Haeckel's when he spoke of a "psychic principle in the atom." With Bergson, of course, the unknown factor is the *élan vital*. Yet though it is unknown and thus far mysterious, Burroughs does not regard the factor as supernatural in origin. To the end, he considers the great service of science—far outweighing any dogmatism that it had developed within itself—to be the freeing of the human mind from irrational bondage to the supernatural. To Burroughs, all things in the universe, all influences and energies, are natural. He is a monist through and through.

IV   Geology: "The Grist of the Gods"

In his later years Burroughs became keenly and profoundly interested in geology. The interest was doubtlessly stimulated by his trips to Alaska and the far West; but, as any geologist knows, this interest also found ample stimulation in Burroughs' own ancient Catskills. Some of the first essays to develop from this new enthusiasm are "The Grist of the Gods" and "The Divine Soil" in *Leaf and Tendril* (1908). Geology to Burroughs was the key to man's understanding of his home, the earth; and it thus served the general function which he always demanded of science—that of aiding man in knowing himself. Most fascinating to him is the paradox geology presents in regard to human origins. The thin film of soil that covers much of the earth is the source of man's bodily existence. Yet it has been formed by death—dead organic matter and the decay of rocks: "The more it is a cemetery, the more it becomes a nursery" (200). Human life is really but an extension of the soil, subject to the same laws that bind it and control the planets and the galaxies. From the same soil, Burroughs ponders, even the soul may have emerged; for matter is ever ready to transform itself into spirit—a process which is continuous and contemporaneous. Man is ever present during the act of divine creation; and, with Whitman, Burroughs believes that the soul of man is not less than his body.

In *Time and Change* (1912) Burroughs' interest in geology finds fuller expression. In his preface he apologizes to the reader for giving him stones when he might prefer bread. But his stones are for the soul, for geology feeds the soul as much as either philosophy or religion. The correct reading of the rocky book of the earth's surface, he explains, has been indispensable to him in the difficult progress toward his own acceptance of the Darwinian doctrine of man's animal origin—a remark difficult to understand, since he seems to have fully accepted Darwin's main conclusions at least as early as 1886. But obviously geology broadened and perhaps strengthened his reliance on the evolutionary theory. At any rate, he states in his preface that he wishes to share his geologically inspired musings and conclusions with his readers.

The opening essay, "The Long Road," which has already been cited, begins with remarks about the awesomeness of the eons of time through which man's evolution has progressed. In this development—impelled by what he calls the "creative energy" (8)—he sees an inevitable chain of cause and effect leading from simplicity to the greatest complexity—a direction of growth that he finds basic to all change. The countless millennia during which the inorganic reigned alone were followed by other countless millennia in which the organic drifted from the insensate to the animate and instinctual and finally, during the last few hours of geological time, emerged into the rational and the spiritual in man. As one reads Burroughs on geology, one is struck by the reverence with which he contemplates these age-old processes which are still going on in the present, and his great merit as a writer in these essays is that he is able to inspire a similar reverence in his reader.

Time and Change contains the essays on the Grand Canyon and the Yosemite already mentioned, which deal with geology in its more spectacular aspects. In another essay, "Through the Eyes of the Geologist," he addresses himself to his own pastoral Catskills, where the soil is deep even on the mountainsides. Surely more suited for human habitation than the rocky canyons and cliffs of the West, they represent to Burroughs more of a culmination in the planet's development. This final chapter of the book of the earth was Burroughs' favorite, for he had lived with it all his life, at first unconsciously—and now consciously—reading its message in the boulders that strewed his father's fields and in the soil's gifts of sustenance, warmth, and shelter. The concept of a vast ice sheet, first postulated by Louis Agassiz, which shaped the landscape and determined the nature of the soil in the northeastern United States fascinated Burroughs as much as the idea of evolution itself. In these late years in his life, while he summered in a renovated farmhouse on the edge of the old farm, he could see the work wrought by the great glacier not only in the miles of stone walls that netted the hillsides but in the sweep and contours of mountain ranges and the shape and direction of the valleys. Looking out on such a scene, he could feel himself in the midst of the eternal changes.

V   *Bergson: Creative Energy*

Henri Bergson, the French philosopher, has been mentioned several times already as contributing to Burroughs' thought on evolution. Burroughs must have read Bergson's *Creative Evolution* (1907) soon after it appeared in English in 1910, for one finds him writing about it in late 1911. So great was his admiration for Bergson that he went to hear him lecture at Columbia University in 1913, though he could not understand a word of the speaker's French. Later he met Bergson at a tea given by Nicholas Murray Butler. Describing the occasion in a letter to his painter friend Orlando Rouland, Burroughs reports that he himself was lionized almost as much as Bergson, who knew Burroughs' work and was extremely cordial. The great German philosopher Rudolph Eucken, also present, was also acquainted with Burroughs' writing.

In Bergson, Burroughs was surprised to find ideas analogous to ones he himself had included in his *Atlantic* essay "Expression" over fifty years earlier. This is to say that he found in Bergson Transcendental ideas—Emersonian and Whitmanian ideas—incorporated into a philosophy of evolution in a manner that Burroughs himself had been striving for and in some degree had already succeeded in developing. He was excited about Bergson because he corroborated and elucidated so many of Burroughs' own thoughts, or half-thoughts. At any rate, the Bergsonian influence was quick to show itself. In *Time and Change* (1912) the essay "The Phantoms Behind Us" (a title drawn appropriately from one of Whitman's evolutionary utterances), Burroughs leans heavily on Bergson's concept of creative energy—the directive force in the universe—in an effort to present the spiritual implications of evolution. Burroughs contends that, when man became aware of the innumerable extinct forms and beings from which the creative energy finally evolved man's form and being, he then realized the fundamental truth that he literally lives, moves, and has his being in God (199). Though Burroughs recognizes that the theory of evolution is not all-inclusive in accounting for universal purposes, it is to him the boldest and most far-reaching concept devised by recent science. When combined with the Bergsonian concept of a creative energy that realizes itself step by step through myriad forms, evolution becomes in its own right a religion—perhaps the most awe-inspiring among all religions. Evolution may have a biochemical basis, but chemistry alone cannot explain it. The concept of creative energy allowed Burroughs to make a synthesis of Transcendentalism and scientific materialism—a synthesis essential to his and, he thought, to man's spiritual well-being. "The body is a machine plus something else" (209), and the "something else" is as much a mystery as the profoundest one of the old religions. It used to be called *God*; Burroughs, since reading Bergson, called it "creative energy." The two may be quite literally equated in all respects.

As in so many matters important to modern man, Whitman, to Burroughs, came closer than any other poet in describing this energy that works within matter: "Urge and urge and urge, always the procreant urge of the world" (213). The source of this urge, or the urge itself, is a God-equivalent for modern man. Rather than stripping man of the need for a belief in God, science, especially evolution, has fortified his conviction that he is subject to something much greater than himself which has predestined his being as the end product of innumerable ages of unceasing, but not directionless, change, in the chemical and physical composition of the universe, the world, and the living forms that inhabit it. Having survived the terrible "hazards of the past," as Burroughs termed the upheavals and cataclysms far back in geological time, man now emerges as the creative energy's "master-piece"—rather "feeble" (223), perhaps, but still more in control of his planet than any other animate creature is. Burroughs considers this emergence to be unexplained by the physical sciences. Man's power of reason and his spiritual rise into a sphere in which he can discern between good and evil make him divine in a unique sense. The creative energy has perhaps come close to duplicating itself in its most complex creation. The Book of Genesis is surely one of the phantoms behind Burroughs' philosophy: God created man in His image.

To Burroughs, it must be repeated, Bergson was carrying on the work of Emerson and Whitman, to whom science was welcome because it supplied a fresh and significant body of symbols whereby they could "indicate the path between reality and men's souls" (Whitman). Similarly Bergson, whose *Creative Evolution* Burroughs believed was "to mark an epoch in the history of modern thought"—a book which "blooms and bears fruit in the spirit to a degree quite unprecedented" (*Summit of the Years*, 72)—built his Transcendental philosophy on modern physical sciences. Indeed, Bergson, when one contrasts his work with the dead weight of Herbert Spencer's mechanistic views of life and the universe, illustrates vividly, as do Emerson and Whitman, the advantages of a marriage of science and poetry, of the intellect and the spirit.

To Burroughs, the strict physico-chemical scientists were hamstring-ing themselves by their refusal to allow for a vital force not explicable by their sciences. Thus, in *The Breath of Life* (1915) Burroughs points out that they sometimes permitted themselves to utter absurdities, as when Haeckel asserted that life arises spontaneously or when Tyndall stated that life is self-evolved. Some sort of vitalism, like that postulated in Bergson's idea of creative energy or the *élan vital*, adapts itself to changing concepts of matter—especially to the atomic theory—much more readily than a doctrinaire mechanistic philosophy. The vitalists have the advantage of enjoying a greater scope for the imagination; they align themselves, though at a distance, with the poets and mystics.

In the essay "The Journeying Atoms" (in *The Breath of Life*), which owes its title to Emerson's "The Shynx"—"Journeying atoms,/Primordial wholes," (189)—Burroughs demonstrates the flexibility of vitalism. All forms of matter are composed ultimately of substances that are actually almost vacuums, namely, the atoms, each of which is made up of varying numbers of electrons whirling around a neutron. Because of easily predictable and observable affinities, these atoms combine into other substances as described by the science of chemistry. Occasionally some of the combinations assume the aspects of life. Chemistry may explain the formation of the compounds that make up the living organism, but it does not explain the activities of living organisms composed of such compounds any more than it does the origin of life. To explain life, another force—natural but not yet understood—must be postulated, as is done in vitalism.

Burroughs explains differing views on the nature and origins of life by taking into account the temperaments of those holding the views. A scientist whose whole career has been devoted to the search for objective truth is clearly going to tend toward a mechanistic philosophy; anything so intangible as vitalism will repel him. The poets, the religious, the meditators, and the artists will be repelled by the mechanical theories of life. Only occasionally, as with Sir Oliver Lodge, whom Burroughs admired, does one find a thinker combining the qualities of a scientist and a philosophical idealist. Yet even some rather hard-headed scientists have not been totally antagonistic toward a nonmaterialistic view. Tyndall, for example, avowed that matter is "at bottom essentially mystical and transcendental" (*The Breath of Life*, 219); and, in an imaginary discussion between Lucretius and Bishop Butler, Tyndall has the latter—expressing his own ideas—question whether out of "dead atoms, sensation, thought, and emotion" may arise or whether one is "likely to extract Homer out of the rattling of dice, or the Differential Calculus out of the clash of billiard balls" (220). Burroughs was also impressed by Tyndall's famous and poetic description of life as a wave journeying through and shaping matter but, owing to the constant loss and gain of molecules in a living body, never for "two consecutive moments of existence . . . composed of the same particles."[4]

All his life Burroughs had considered himself a literary man rather than a scientist. His was the "freer view of the open-air naturalist and literary philosopher" (257). His sympathies were with men like Bergson and Sir Oliver Lodge who regard life as "some mysterious entity in itself, existing apart from the matter which it animates and uses; not a source of energy but a timer and releaser of energy" (237). Admittedly, such suppositions are in the realm of philosophy; but to Burroughs philosophy, not science, came to grips with fundamental problems.

VI   *Cosmic Mind*

Analogous to creative energy, in Burroughs' philsophy, is what he termed "cosmic mind." The creative energy—the *élan vital*—is a force, or a factor, infusing matter and directing it into more and more complex forms of life. The cosmic mind, the intelligence that underlies that force, is difficult to separate from it; but the cosmic mind is sufficiently a distinct aspect of the force to warrant Burroughs' discussion. Doubtlessly Burroughs' notion of the cosmic mind is an outgrowth of Emerson's concept of the "oversoul," which it closely resembles. As has been seen, Burroughs considers all of nature, inorganic and organic, as expressions of the cosmic mind; and man is the fullest such expression. In the essay "Untaught Wisdom" in *The Summit of the Years* (1913), Burroughs presents his theory in detail.

His contention is that all nature "is pervaded with mind or mind-stuff" (206). As it operates in vegetable and in lower animate forms of life and even, as physical and chemical law, in all matter, this universal mind is mechanical to the extent that it is not subject to the will or the self-conscious direction of any individual organism. Even the more complex organisms are as "sleep-walkers" so far as awareness of themselves, of their aims, or of their actions is concerned. But with man it is different. In perhaps the boldest speculative passage ever to come from his pen, Burroughs writes:

Is not man's wisdom also older than himself? Is not every pound of force that he uses through his own members or . . . the mechanisms that he invents, a part of the sum total of the force of the universe? In like manner, may we not infer that every spark of intelligence he shows, or is capable of showing, is a part of, or a manifestation of, the intelligence that pervades all things? As he modifies and uses the cosmic force through his various mechanical devices, so the cosmic intelligence is modified and individualized through his reason and personality. The inorganic intelligence of universal nature, so to speak, becomes organic intelligence in the realm of life, appearing in the lower orders in what we call instinct, and in man as self-knowledge and the higher consciousness. (207)

As he grew older, Burroughs, with the help of Bergson, was more and more deeply entrenching himself in the Transcendental thought that he had first learned from Emerson and Whitman; for he had never actually wavered in the conviction that all matter is a manifestation of mind and is pervaded by mind. Burroughs pursued this subject in his next book, *The Breath of Life* (1915), with considerable repetition of the ideas he had previously developed but with a few new approaches worth noting. For example, the scientific "paradox . . . that matter and electricity are one . . ." (48-49) suggests to him Whitman's paradox "that the soul and body are one" (48). In no phase of his career does Burroughs ever drift far from the poets, nor does he lose his sense of the importance of analogies in explaining the abstract and the spiritual world. Thus, he likens the cooperation and specialization of the cells that make up living bodies—liver cells, kidney cells, brain cells, and so on—to the bees in a hive, where the worker bees, the drones, the queen, though all separate beings, labor spontaneously and with one mind—the Spirit of the Hive, as Maurice Maeterlinck called it—in the common effort of keeping alive their closely knit organization. Just as in the hive, or for that matter in a flock of birds, a school of fish, or a human mob, there is in the multicellular organism an intangible something, perhaps unconscious mind, that supersedes the individual cell and holds it and its fellows to their places and functions in the whole.

To Burroughs, it is inconceivable that this force could be merely physical or chemical. In support of his belief he alludes to the findings of Dr. Alexis Carrel of the Rockefeller Institute that the cells live after the body as a whole is dead: "It seems a legitimate inference from this fact that the human body is the organ or instrument of some agent that is not of the body . . . quite independent of the man himself" (98-99). However, Burroughs does not postulate, on the strength of such phenomena, the existence of a God outside of and above nature. Rather, the agent must be inherent in matter as the vital force—here used almost synonymously with "cosmic mind"—which is "potential in matter" (102), not extraneous to it. In this sense, he may speak of the universe as "permeated with spirit" (102), and he is back again to Whitman and Emerson. Or in Goethe's phrase, matter is "the living garment of God" (111), if one regards God as the spiritual component of nature.

In the final essay in *The Breath of Life*, titled "The Naturalist's View of Life," Burroughs summarizes his thought on the cosmic mind. But first he denies that he scorns science; on the contrary, he considers science to be "the redeemer of the physical world" (269) since it reveals the world's beauty and its infinity. But dogmatic science thus far has been unable satisfactorily to deal with the phenomenon of life—satisfactorily, that is, to the idealistic or artistic mind. Man is as natural to the earth "as the rains, the dews, the flowers . . ." (272-73); yet one cannot conceive of him, or life in any form, as being solely the product of physico-chemical forces. Perhaps, as a hangover from Calvinism, man feels dead matter must be breathed upon by the Divine—redeemed from its state of death and sin—before it can be endowed with life—"the doctrine of Paul carried into the processes of nature" (279).

While Burroughs subscribes to no such theological explanation, his philosophy of vitalism needs some creative cosmic principle not yet discovered or admitted by the biochemists: "No cell-analysis will give the secret; no chemical conjuring with the elements will reveal why in the one case they build up a head of cabbage, and in the other a head of Plato" (279). Yet, he always insists, man need not fall back on the supernatural. Emerson's dictum, "When the half-gods go, the gods arrive," need not hold here. Since intelligence evolves out of matter, Burroughs believes intelligence must always have been latent in matter. So must the spiritual and esthetic values of man have sprung from a similar latency—however radically they set man apart from the other forms of life. Man is part of the universe; he can contain nothing that is not inherent in it.

VII   *The Cosmic Chill*

Burroughs' preoccupation with such concepts as those of the cosmic mind and creative energy intensified as old age brought him closer to death. Like most men of sensitivity, he had always thought about death; and as early as 1854, in his seventeenth year, one finds him stating in his notebook that there is "no death, but transition. Every end forms the beginning of something else." Later, he expresses the same thought metaphorically—"death is a phase of life, a redistributing of the [printer's] type"—and as a paradox worthy of Thoreau—"decay is another kind of growth" (*Time and Change*, 259). But when death struck among his family and friends, he found little comfort in such apothegms.

Indeed, Burroughs recognized that he was subject to far more than the normal pain occasioned by bereavement, and his letters and diaries contain many poignant records of his grief. As has been noticed, he grieved long over Whitman's death—a sorrow that had a positively unhinging effect and made him for the rest of his life even more conscious of death than he had previously been. The most distressing thing about grief with him was its duration. After his father died, he wrote in a letter to Myron Benton that his sorrow was "not of the desirable kind" but like his "seasickness, not so severe as with some, but ... apt to last the whole voyage."[5] Each year he would visit the family graves in Roxbury as if under a compulsion to renew his pain; and in his diary for 1920, one finds a moving notation about the last of these cemetery visits before his own death: "Visit the graves of my dead in the Old Yellow Church burying-ground, and in the Presbyterian burying-ground in the village. I stood long and long at Father's and Mother's graves, and seemed very near them. And at the grave of dear Channy B. [Deyo] ... I lingered about them all, and said goodbye to them all, and said I would come again if I lived."[6] Channy (Chauncey) B. Deyo was a favorite nephew who had died of brain disease forty-six years earlier—a loss from which, as one sees here, Burroughs never totally recovered. It was a marvel to him that humanity had learned to live wih the thought of death.

Burroughs' brooding on death is part of his general longing for a lost past—part of his homesickness. At the family graves he is lamenting his own boyhood and youth as much as his departed kinsmen. In a letter to Myron Benton in 1893, he writes: "The solitude of life increases ... ; the shadows are a little deeper and longer as the sun creeps down the sky. The night cometh and is not afar off."[7] And later in the same year he writes to Benton that "gone," "gone," is written on every field of the Old Farm, and he describes himself as living "in the past amid old scenes."[8]

As for the teachings of orthodox religion on the subject of death and immortality, Burroughs is unimpressed. In his essay "Analogy— True and False" in *Literary Values* (1902), he seems to go out of his way to attack some of the usual arguments for survival of the soul. He believes that St. Paul, when he likens the dead body to a seed, is making an invalid analogy; for the seed is not dead; it is merely dormant. Similarly, Bishop Butler's analogy of death to sleep is ineffective since the states of the body in death and sleep are utterly different. Other, and more valid, analogies, he goes on to say in this same essay (which, though on a rhetorical matter, switches to the subject of mortality), point to nothingness after death. "Out of this whirling, seething, bubbling universe of warring and clashing forces man has emerged" (*Literary Values*, 39), and one may be reasonably sure that man as a species will continue to exist for some time longer. "But as to the future of the individual ... what are we safe in affirming? Only this—that as we had a beginning we shall have an ending; that as yesterday we were not, so to-morrow we shall not be. A man is like the electric spark that glows and crackles for an instant between two dark, silent, inscrutable eternities. . . . Darkness and silence before; darkness and silence after. I do not say this is the summing up of the whole question of immortality. I only mean to say that this is where the argument from analogy lands us" (39-40).

But actually this statement *is* a summing up of his thinking on the subject, at least until shortly before his own death. The universe described by the natural sciences simply offered no assurance of personal immortality. On this one point, much to his own regret, he differed from his beloved Whitman. When Burroughs refers to death as a "transition" or a "redistribution of type," he is thinking of the disintegration of organic matter into its constituent atoms and molecules, which reform once again, in the eternal cycles of dying and rebirth, in other living organisms—a process that obviously does not require the survival of an individual consciousness. In a universe like ours without the certainty of future existence, a man's life follows a course of inexorably intensifying isolation. All the associations of his earlier years desert him, prove to be different from what he thought them, cease to serve as a protection from "the great cosmic void that encompasses [him] " (266), and finally engulfs him. Inevitably with this sense of isolation in a seemingly indifferent universe, comes the "cosmic chill" (*The Light of Day*, 133).

All Burroughs' life, but in his later years especially, he was at great pains to erect shelters against the cosmic chill, not by self-delusion but by cultivating friendships, by immersing himself in the beauties of nature, and above all by developing a philosophy that would provide some warmth without outraging his reason. Like any intellectually honest man, he was only partially successful in his efforts. In his final speculations, found in *Accepting the Universe* (1920) and published the year before his death, he finds, while searching for useful analogies, one that had hitherto escaped him. Starting with the principle of the persistence of energy, he wonders if consciousness, which T. H. Huxley accorded a reality equal to that of matter and energy, or the principle of vitality, which may share a like reality, may not survive the death of the body. By analogy with energy, it could be surmised that both *might* persist; but Burroughs does no more than state the possibility. The great questions are: Will personal identity remain? Are men's souls immortal as constituted in this life? "There is comfort in the thought that if there is no immortality, we shall not know it" (*Accepting the*

Universe, 287). Yet he agrees with Whitman that death cannot be an evil because it is in accord with nature; and, as Marcus Aurelius said, "Nothing is evil which is according to nature" (120). Such confidence is based on the belief that the cosmic mind knows what it is doing. The cosmic mind was, therefore, Burroughs' antidote to the cosmic chill.

VIII   *Theology and Religion*

One must always remember that Burroughs was reared in a strictly Calvinistic, fundamentalist family. In *The Light of Day* (1900) he presents his thoughts on his ancestral religion and suggests some appropriate substitutes. In it, he explores orthodoxy in the light of present-day science, much to the damage of the established faiths. In his arrangement and selection of material, especially in the first pages of the book, Burroughs provides some hints as to the major phases of his own spiritual development. The opening essay, "A Retrospect," describes his earliest memories of his father, an Old School Baptist, angrily arguing on the subject of free will with a Methodist neighbor. Neither man was educated beyond the ability to spell out the Bible and perhaps the pages of a religious magazine. But both had fixed ideas on theology. Burroughs' father, of course, argued in favor of predestination—the doctrine so basic to the creed of his Connecticut forefathers. To him, Methodism was soft, effete, with its salvation for all who strove for it and with its rejection of the doctrine of election; the Old School Baptists were manning the last bastion of Calvinism. Of course, neither man in the dispute ever conceded the fraction of a point, but Burroughs was more attracted to the clement God of the neighbor than to the harsh and rigid one of his father. Methodism, though gentler, was still as impossible as Calvinism for Burroughs, in his later years, to accept. Both were founded on unbending dogma which tended to produce in its adherents a sour fanaticism rather than a sweet reasonableness.

What repelled Burroughs in the dogmatic religions was their complexity. Though he grants that his father and the neighbor got great comfort from their respective religions—he even envies them their faith—he considers their theology to have been cluttered with nonessentials. To be truly inward and deeply felt, a religion must be relatively uncluttered. The inwardness of religion is a theme that Burroughs dwells on as a part of the simplification of religion—its reduction from multiplicity to unity. All of real importance that occurs in religion occurs inwardly; the rest is either mythology—like the doctrine of vicarious sacrifice, the story of the fall of Adam and Eve, or the theory of conversion through divine grace—or it is sheer legalism, the peculiar mark of Calvin. Because of the light of science, theology is gradually decaying, as Burroughs maintains in the essay "The Decadence of Theology," along with other matters of mere credulity, such as spirit-rapping, witchcraft, charms, and incantations. With the loss of theology may come the "cosmic chill" to newly enlightened minds, but the chill need be only temporary, and the ensuing faith may be stronger than the usurped one. The monstrous God of the forefathers, whose only desire was to be propitiated by his groveling creatures, can be supplanted by a more reassuring sense of man's immersion in the oneness of nature.

But, along with this sense of unity, must be a feeling of the wonder and the mystery of the universe; for awe is as much a necessity for the expression of the religious sentiment as is a conviction of the brotherhood of man. "Here is this vast congeries of vital forces which we call Nature, regardless of time because it has all time, regardless of waste because it is the All, regardless of space because it is infinite, regardless of man because man is a part of it, regardless of life because it is the sum total of life, gaining what it spends, conserving what it destroys, always young, always old, reconciling all contradictions—the sum and synthesis of all powers and qualities, infinite and incomprehensible. This is all the God we can know, and this we cannot help but know. We want no evidence of this God . . ." (*The Light of Day*, 188). This universe is what man is a part of when he is dead as well as when he is alive. After death, the particles that made up his body, as well as the life principle (this was written years before Bergson had published *Creative Evolution*) that animated him, will be absorbed back into the All. Consciousness, Burroughs believed at this time, will be extinguished—and this will be distressing to man—but man must take comfort in the fact that he has immortality in the deathlessness of all nature, not in the perpetuation of his own individual identity.

It is not surprising that at this point in his exposition Burroughs quotes from Emerson's "Brahma" and, elsewhere, from *The Bhagavad-Gita*. Like so many of the twentieth century and the nineteenth—Dreiser and Whitman, for example—who reasoned themselves into a scientific or Transcendental monism, Burroughs found himself in accord with the description of the universe found in the Hindu *Upanishads*. Especially interesting is the comparison with Dreiser, who in his book of essays, *Hey-Rub-a-Dub-Dub*, wrote of the "mystery and wonder of life" as revealed by science, but somewhat later, in *The*

Stoic, presented a Hindu view of the cosmos. Although Dreiser visited Slabsides at the time Burroughs was preparing *The Light of Day* for publication, one would be rash to claim an influence from Burroughs on Dreiser, who switched only in later years from a strict materialism to a species of mysticism. There is, however, a startling parallelism in their intellectual development: both came from rigidly orthodox Christian homes; both had been fascinated by science, which had undermined their inherited religions; both had felt the cosmic chill; and both found refuge from it in a religion of nature. Burroughs assures the reader that "we are not detached, cut off, by all these billions of miles of space, but still as close and dependent as the fruit that hangs to the branch" (249), and he concludes that there is a measureless spiritual significance in the natural grandeur—the air, the earth, the water—that enfolds man. So Dreiser, too, in *The Bulwark*, as well as in *The Stoic*, reverts to a nature mysticism that is a far cry from the harsh deterministic naturalism of his earlier books, though even in *The Financier* and *The Titan* Cowperwood's feelings of awe, inspired by the stars in infinite space, presage Dreiser's later outlook.

As for worship, Burroughs asserts in *Accepting the Universe* (1920) that he feels no more duty toward God than he feels toward the law of gravity. He considers himself an integral part of the Eternal, not a chattel of it. He is happy to be alive in this world of which he is a part rather than an intruder. He is "a handful of the dust of the cosmos" (52), part and parcel of the universal scheme of things. Whatever there is of heaven is here and now, not in the Promised Land of the theologians, who Burroughs thinks have "blackened and defaced our earthly temple" (53). Men share in "the universal beneficence" (54), which directs things for its own ends, which may not be solely man's ends but ones in which he shares. All the "good" and "evil" man sees in himself are shared by the Eternal as well; when he sees them operative on a cosmic scale, he calls the "good" God and the "evil" the devil. Even Emerson has fallen into the anthropomorphism of referring to the "unscrupulousness of nature." Among the poets, Whitman alone consistently recognized evil as part, or a manifestation, of the One—which accounts for his equalizing "good" and "evil" in his poetry. However, Burroughs insists that, so far as man's own actions are concerned, man must obey the moral law of which he alone is the receptacle.

In "The Faith of a Naturalist," a summary of his views in *Accepting the Universe*, Burroughs emphasizes that man—by identifying himself with nature and by realizing that he is a part of nature and that all the currents of the universe flow through him—can achieve a truly religious position. Burroughs would concur with Wallace Stevens' statement in "Sunday Morning": the wholly divine Jove no longer satisfies man's religious craving, nor does the half-divine Jesus. God has now become wholly man, man as part of nature. In agreement with Stevens, Burroughs describes what a truly religious experience for modern man must be: "Amid the decay of creeds, love of nature has high religious value. . . . Every walk to the woods is a religious rite, every bath in the stream is a saving ordinance. Communion service is at all hours . . . (116-17). Yet, though Burroughs thinks that nature-worship has saved many persons "from mammon-worship" (116), he does not insist on the sole efficacy of his religious views. Religion, he believes, is a feeling; and, if the feeling is present, the validity is of secondary importance.

IX   *Good and Evil*

The problem of the seeming coexistence of good and evil in the universal order gave Burroughs serious pause, as is bound to be the case with any monist. As has been seen, he described in his earliest nature essays not only the songbirds and their nests but also the snakes that robbed the nests. He was never one to close his eyes to the ugly and evil that are always to be found side by side with the beautiful and the good. As for finding God in nature, it is just as easy to find the devil in nature, for to whom else can man ascribe the incidence of floods, earthquakes, hurricanes? But, as a monist, Burroughs cannot tolerate the dualism implied in the recognition of the devil in the universe. The trouble, he decides, stems from man's instinctive tendency to invent an anthropormorphic God: what is good for man must be good for the entire universe; therefore, God is only good. Burroughs is quick to point out the error of this approach. What is good for a typhoid bacillus or a cancer is assuredly not good for man; yet the cancer and the bacillus are as much a part of nature as is man. When someone asked John Muir what poison ivy was good for, he answered that perhaps it was good for itself.

In *Leaf and Tendril* (1908), the essay "All's Right With the World" contains a statement which Burroughs considers correct if the world is intellectually considered: "To the seeing mind nature presents a series, an infinite series, of logical sequences; cause and effect are inseparably joined, and things could in no wise be other than what they are" (263).

But considered from the moral point of view, all is not right with the world; man is appalled by the evil, pain, and destruction that beset him on every side. How to reconcile these two verdicts, one of the mind, the other of the heart? In an attempt at reconciliation, Burroughs establishes a strange dichotomy. "Man's intellect," he asserts, "is from God, his moral nature is the work of his own hands" (266)—it is something he has developed in the evolutionary process as distinctly his own that is not shared with the rest of the universe. Man's "reason is reflected in the course of nature; it is in unison with the cosmic process; it looks upon the world and says it is good. . . . But his moral nature is not reflected in the objective world. . . . There is only law which knows no mercy, or tenderness, or forgiveness, or self-sacrifice, and which is oblivious to pain and suffering. Hence the God which our moral nature demands is not found in the world . . ." (266). The true, the only, God is the one that works through the universal laws of nature, and he is an amoral God.

Man's moral sense—an outcome of the evolutionary struggle upward —is indeed a part of the order of things. It serves a purpose in that it keeps man from destroying himself, as he could easily do if there were no check, for example, to his combative tendencies. But the reason cannot consider the moral sense as the *only* beneficent force; in fact, it is an outcome of what man considers to be evil. Man need not, and if he is to survive, must not accept the evils of the world—the things and forces that threaten his existence, whether they are inside or outside himself. His struggle against them is part of the struggle for survival. But, on the level of reason, he should not rail against these "evils" as defects in God's plan for the cosmos. Evil is from God just as good is. In truth, "all's right with the world" (272).

Like Robinson Jeffers, Burroughs refused to judge the universe solely by human values; but, unlike Jeffers, he regarded the slow, painful evolution of the human race as important to the universe—as beneficial in the sense that humanity is a supreme manifestation of nature's plan. Humanity's moral and esthetic values, so recently evolved, are as much a biological law as is that of the survival of the fittest. Moral values, indeed, as has been noted, are necessary for the survival of the race and must be applied—as they have hitherto not been—to the relationship of nations if mankind is not to be destroyed; and World War I offered sufficient evidence of this need. Man, Burroughs insists, must obey his specially evolved moral law, even if it does not embrace the entire universe.

X *Freedom of the Will*

When Burroughs suggested that the presence of evil in the world actually serves the inscrutable purpose of the Eternal, he had circled curiously around to the orthodox Calvinist belief that God has his reasons, which man is not to question, for permitting the devil some latitude of activity. Another question that engrossed Burroughs' attention during his life was that of the freedom of the will, which in its relation to the doctrines of predestination and election was also a problem of perennial interest to the Calvinists. In Burroughs' writings there are more references to it than to any other theological or philosophical matter. It is worthwhile to trace his efforts to unravel this knot in terms of his overall Transcendental monism.

Simply stated, the question is this: Does a person have control over his choices as to his actions and over the carrying out of these choices, or is he under a necessity predestined by God or determined by natural law to choose and act in a certain manner and no other? From Augustine through Calvin a large sector of Christian theology taught that man probably can act as he chooses but that his choices are predetermined by his temperament, which is in turn determined by God. After Adam, all men are fallen and naturally choose evil and enjoy a limited capability of translating these evil choices into action. If a person is among those chosen to be saved, according to the doctrine of election, he will become capable of choosing and carrying out good actions. If he is among the damned, his choices and actions will always be evil. Whether he is one of the elect or one of the damned is predestined by God according to God's eternal decree. The individual has absolutely no initiatory control over his damnation or his salvation. According to the doctrine of predestination, all man's efforts to lead a good life need not result in conversion, which is the signal that one may be among the saved, though such efforts are encouraged.

The scientific determinists of the nineteenth century—men like Ernst Heinrich Haeckel and Herbert Spencer, to whose thought Burroughs was fully exposed—allowed for even less freedom of choice and will than the Calvinists. They envisaged what William James called a block universe, a vast mechanical-chemical apparatus in which humanity and individual persons were mere cogs acting and choosing actions in accordance with the physical and biochemical laws that controlled them. As one French philosopher put it, an individual had no more control over his destiny than do the stones in a road. Man, a blob of matter like any other object, is subject to the same laws as is matter. His racial and individual heredity and his environment hold him in an unbreakable clutch against which what he likes to call his will is pitiably impotent.

Burroughs' first contact with the problem of the freedom of the will, as has been noted, was in his family's kitchen where he heard his father excitedly arguing in favor of predestination against the, to him, heretical views of a Methodist neighbor. The first record of Burroughs' own opinions on the subject occur in the Notebooks of 1859, in which, at the age of twenty-two, he writes: "Every man by obeying his own law, or the promptings of his own being, obeys a higher law. . . ." The emphasis on law echoes Calvinism—though by this time Burroughs had rejected his father's orthodoxy—in that it implies that a man's temperament as God decreed it to be governs his choices. Yet the equal emphasis on obeying indicates the possibility of disobeying, which would be impossible from the Calvinistic viewpoint. Later in the same Notebook he seems to swing entirely over to the Calvinist position, probably unknowingly, when he bluntly states: "Inward law is fate; outward is free will." In other words, men have what they have inside them; and they direct this outward, translate it into action, by their own volitions. They will their actions in accordance with their own unchangeable temperament, which inevitably must govern the direction of their wishes.

Four years later in a letter to Myron Benton, Burroughs praises David Wasson's view on the will as stated in an article, "Mr. Buckle as a Thinker," published in the *Atlantic Monthly* of January, 1863. Wasson was distressed with Buckle's denial on scientific grounds of any freedom of the will; according to Buckle, what men call freedom is merely chance, identical with chance occurrences in the physical world. Wasson counters: "To assert the identity of chance and free-will is but another way of saying that pure freedom is one and the same with absolute lawlessness,—that where freedom exists, law, order, reason do not."[9] Wasson then asserts that man's will is free and that it is an expression of the divine Reason—a Transcendental explanation, but one that carries with it its own difficulties.

Emerson also had grappled with the enigma in *Conduct of Life* (1860) in the essay "Fate," with which Burroughs surely was familiar: "He who sees through the design, presides over it, and must will that which must be. We sit and rule, and, though we sleep, our dream will come to pass. Our thought, though it were only an hour old, affirms an oldest necessity, not to be separated from thought, and not to be separated from will. They must always have coexisted. . . . It is not mine or thine, but the will of all mind."[10] Later in the essay Emerson adds, "The tendency of every man to enact all that is in his constitution is expressed in the old belief that the efforts which we make to escape from our destiny only serve to lead us into it."[11]

If, as Wasson states, man's will is an expression of divine reason, then Emerson's conclusion would seem to apply more logically than Wasson's conclusion that the will is entirely free. Be that as it may, Burroughs could find food for thought on the subject in both Wasson, who bravely asserted the will's freedom, and Emerson, who conceded to it only that freedom—which seemed not much—that it shared as part of the cosmic will. Burroughs' final views on the matter are strongly tinged with scientific determinism; heredity and physical and social environment enthrall the will. But, as he indicates in a late essay, "Fated to Be Free," in *Under the Apple-Trees* (1916), he also shares Emerson's opinion that men will what their human nature, whether individually or collectively considered, induces them to will. They will what their most basic tendencies, which they share with nature, require them to will. Ultimately, since nature is directed by the cosmic mind, they will what the cosmic mind directs. They have the illusion of freedom, Burroughs thinks, because they will as they like; but they do not have control over what they like—a thought which, along with Emerson's, smacks strongly of Jonathan Edwards' conclusions and reflects both Emerson's and Burroughs' Calvinistic roots. Ultimately, to Burroughs, men are shackled to the needs of the creative energy in its evolutionary development of the species man.

The same paradox is at the heart of both Transcendentalism and Calvinism: each requires exertion of the individual will in the attainment of salvation, and each places the directing of the individual will under a higher one beyond the individual's control. Thus each has a built-in tendency toward Quietism, passivity. Why strenuously exert ourselves to exercise a will that a higher power is going to direct anyway? Burroughs expresses this passivity in the lap of the All in his most popular poem, "Waiting," written in 1862 in the first full flush of Emerson's influence on him. One stanza reads:

> I stay my haste, I make delays,
>   For what avails this eager pace?
> I stand amid the eternal ways,
>   And what is mine shall know my face.[12]

Interestingly, the third and fourth lines of the stanza are engraved on the plaque that marks Burroughs' grave in a field on the home farm in Roxbury.

But at least Emerson's and Burroughs' ideas on the will do not concur with those of the scientific determinists, who reduce man to a machine. To both Emerson and Burroughs, the direction of the will is derived from the spirit shared by man rather than from material force or chance. Without backing away from any of the rapidly multiplying findings of science, Burroughs managed to keep alive this important aspect of Transcendentalism—the idea of God and divine will in man.

A cogent statement of Burroughs' position on the will is in a letter, hitherto unpublished, to Albert B. Paine, the friend and biographer of Mark Twain. Paine had apparently written to ask Burroughs to comment on the matter of predestination; his doing so may have arisen from the fact that Mark Twain was a confirmed determinist, or fatalist, as is evidenced in several of his works, but most notably in the rather sophomoric dialogue *What Is Man?*, which reduces man to an automaton. The date of the letter is missing, but it must have been written in 1913, for Bergson's presence at Columbia University is mentioned, and he was there three years after Mark Twain's death. Burroughs writes in part:

I fear I cannot crack that predestination nut this morning, which you seem to have disposed of. It is indeed a hard one. Necessity [determinism] rules dead matter [in his Diary for August 10, 1898, Burroughs had written: "There is no such thing as change. . . . All events are determined by law."[13]], but I try to make myself believe that in life, in spirit there is some freedom, some choice. If you haven't read Bergson's *Creative Evolution* I think you will be glad to have done so. It is a wonderful book from the literary point of view, and as philosophy, it limbers up the stiff old universe in a remarkable way. It takes the starch out of predestinationism, or the mechanistic conception of life, and shows evolution to be something more than the result of the laws of mechanical necessity. I am sure Mark Twain would have enjoyed it. There is no escape from iron fate if you follow the logic of the scientific intellect, but Bergson appeals to a higher court. He shows convincingly how the logical intellect cannot grasp the true meaning of life, or of the evolutionary process.[14]

To the end Burroughs remained true to the philosophy of Emerson and Whitman—the philosophy of the transcendence of spirit over matter.

CHAPTER 6

Last Years and Reputation

I *Zenith of Popularity*

DURING the last twenty years of his life, Burroughs became a celebrity. Popular as a writer of nature essays since the 1860s, when the first of these pieces began to appear in the *Atlantic Monthly* and other periodicals, he soon became known and respected as a literary critic as well, especially for his enthusiastic promotion of Walt Whitman. Finally, with the publication of the essays that later made up *The Light of Day* (1900), he established himself as an authoritative interpreter of science in its relation to theology and philosophy. Almost from the beginning his writing had been in demand, and in the last three decades the editors clamored for his work. There was hardly a magazine of general circulation of his times that did not issue essays by him. The *Atlantic*, three years after its first number in 1857, published his "Expression" and continued to accept his writing for sixty-one years. Burroughs had become so prestigious that he was constantly requested to write introductions for various publishing ventures, from a series of nature books to selections of Walt Whitman's poetry. Ginn and Company offered to make him a fortune if he would turn to writing textbooks, but he refused, saying Thoreaulike that he had no need of a fortune. Newspaper reporters sought him out for interviews and statements on the secrets of his longevity and success. He was named in advertisements as the sponsor of a patent medicine. He was now the Seer of Slabsides, and his woodland retreat had become somewhat less than a hermitage, what with the continuous repair there of the outer world—Vassar College girls on nature tours, friends and the merely curious, and even a president and a candidate for the presidency of the United States.

There were many reasons for this remarkable popularity aside from Burroughs' very real merits as writer, naturalist, critic, and philosopher. As already mentioned, the use of his essays as school texts since 1887 had familiarized generations of children with his name, so that on his trip to Yellowstone with Theodore Roosevelt he received, at times, nearly as much acclaim as did the president. Of course, his association with Roosevelt on this and other occasions and their partnership in the nature-faker controversy could result only in added prestige for Burroughs with the public. Simultaneously, his acquaintance among famous men multiplied to include Harvey Firestone, Thomas Edison, and Henry Ford. With these three he took motor-camping trips—covered by the press—through New England and the South. Ford especially became a close friend. He gave Burroughs several Model T cars, which the recipient, in his seventies, learned to drive at great peril to himself and his friends; he financed journeys and vacations for Burroughs; and he paid for the clearing by dynamite of a stony field at the old farm and at one point bought the farm itself and gave it to Burroughs.

Burroughs accepted these favors from Ford as he had those from Harriman and Roosevelt, with neither ingratitude nor groveling humility. He himself had never attempted to become wealthy. He had farmed and written and worked for the government to earn a living adequate for his rather simple tastes. Only after the age of sixty was he able to exist by his writing alone. If men like Ford, who had found their fulfillment in accumulating millions, wished to spend their money on him, he would let no false pride on his part prevent them. Though he had a Yankee farmer's sense of the worth of a dollar, money never became a symbol of self-esteem for him. He always gave most generously and he was willing to receive from people who were kindly disposed toward him.

In many ways, though he liked Ford, Burroughs was highly critical of him. Thus, when Ford announced that Burroughs' writing was superior to that of any other author who had ever lived, Burroughs remarked that Ford had extremely bad taste in literature and the arts, as evidenced in his preference of photographs to even the most skillfully painted portraits. The most appealing and approving glimpse of Ford that Burroughs presents is a description of him in his shirt-sleeves on a southern tour fixing their car after a garage mechanic had given up on it. Here was Ford doing what he really knew how to do—not expatiating on art, history, and sociology.

Burroughs' association with industrial magnates and others of immense power and wealth may well have damaged his reputation with the rather large segment of the postwar intelligentsia who were more or less in rebellion against the establishment and its values. Actually, all his life, Burroughs had many more friends among artists and fellow writers than he did among the moneyed and powerful. As he grew older, his patriarchal mien with its Whitmanesque beard made him a favorite subject for painters and sculptors. One artist, his close friend Orlando Rouland, did thirteen portraits of him. Recognition from the more conventional intellectual community come to him with election to the American Academy of Arts and Letters and with honorary degrees from Yale, Colgate, and the University of Georgia. He turned down others.

When John Burroughs died in 1921 while crossing Ohio in a railroad train on his way home from California, the event made the front pages and occasioned many eulogistic editorials. Almost at once his friends formed a John Burroughs Memorial Association, still active and centered in New York in the American Museum of Natural History, where there is a special Burroughs exhibit. Among the association's functions is the awarding annually of a medal to the author of the best volume of nature writing of the year. Lucius Beebe, Joseph Wood Krutch, and Rachel Carson have been recipients. Other Burroughs clubs, devoted mainly to conservation and nature study, are located elsewhere in the country. A very active one is at Burroughs' home town of Roxbury, New York. Woodchuck Lodge, Slabsides, and the Bark Study on the Riverby grounds have been named National Historic Landmarks by the Department of the Interior; and the Memorial Field on the old farm, where Burroughs is buried, is maintained by the New York State Department of Environmental Conservation. All of these places are visited by sightseers and Burroughs devotees in large numbers each year.

But Burroughs' books have not fared so well. When he died, they were available in two uniform editions—the regular trade or Riverside edition and the so-called Riverby Edition, which was illustrated, printed on high-quality paper, and handsomely bound in blue with gilt lettering. But for years all his books have been out of print and not until 1968 were reissued (by a reprint house). A collection of excerpts from his work, edited by Farida Wiley, was published in 1954 under the title of *John Burroughs' America*, and in 1969 there appeared a collection of Burroughs' outdoor essays under the title *John Burroughs in Field and Wood*, edited and illustrated with drawings by his granddaughter, Elizabeth Burroughs Kelley. Burroughs has in the past been well represented in anthologies of American literature but, in recent years, with decreasing frequency and quantity.

II   *Literary Reputation*

Critical articles on Burroughs, aside from book reviews, began to appear early in his career. The first of real importance was written by Joel Benton, Myron Benton's brother, and published in *Scribner's Magazine* in 1877. In it Burroughs was favorably compared with Emerson and Thoreau. Others followed, but the zenith was reached in an article titled "Fifty Years of John Burroughs," by Dallas Lore Sharp, in the *Atlantic Monthly* of November, 1910. Commemorating the fiftieth anniversary of the publication of Burroughs' "Expression," this essay pays a rare tribute to a man who had subscribed to the *Atlantic* continuously from its first number, had written regularly for it since its sixth volume, and had regarded it as "his university."[1] The editors gave Dallas Lore Sharp free rein. He placed Burroughs' nature books at the head of their genre, "the most complete, the most revealing, of all our outdoor literature. . . . The essay whose matter is nature, whose moral is human, whose manner is strictly literary, belongs to Mr. Burroughs" (632-35). Burroughs "has turned a little of the universe into literature"; the prose in "The Flight of the Eagle" and in "A River View" is "as perfect, in its way, as anything that has ever been done—single, simple, beautiful in form, and deeply significant" (641).

The first book-length study of Burroughs, published in 1912, was R. J. H. De Loach's *Rambles with John Burroughs*, a volume of appreciative thoughts and reminiscences. A second book was Clara Barrus' *Our Friend John Burroughs*, which appeared in 1914. Though marred by a somewhat uncritical adulation, this volume did contain much interesting and useful biographical material, some of it in the form of autobiographical sketches by Burroughs himself. Dr. Clara Barrus, a psychiatrist at the State Hospital in Middletown, New York, and long an admirer of Burroughs' work, had visited him at Slabsides in 1901. The acquaintance developed into a close friendship, and eventually Dr. Barrus moved to a house on the grounds of Riverby, where for a while the aging Burroughs and his ailing wife lived with her. During the twenty years of their friendship, Clara Barrus served as Burroughs' companion both at home and on his travels, as his physician, and as his typist, editor, and proofreader. So useful was she to him that his literary output markedly increased and did not let up until his death. Fifteen of his twenty-seven books were published during the years—about one-third of his writing career—when she was helping him.

In addition to the secretarial and editorial aid that she gave him, Dr.

Barrus did much to promote Burroughs' reputation. Having assumed the role of his Boswell, she soon set about gathering biographical material in the form of letters and papers and from conversations with him. In addition to *Our Friend John Burroughs*, she published another book on him during his lifetime—*John Burroughs Boy and Man* (1920), which was originally intended to be a boys' book but ended as something much more ambitious, and as suitable for adults as for boys. After Burroughs' death, having been named his literary executor in his will, she brought out two posthumous collections of his essays written, for the most part, during the past several years. One of these, *Under the Maples*, appeared in 1921; and the other, *The Last Harvest*, the following year. In 1925 she published the two-volume "definitive" biography, *The Life and Letters of John Burroughs*, which was followed by a selection from the diaries and notebooks, *The Heart of Burroughs's Journals* in 1928 and by *Whitman and Burroughs Comrades* in 1931.

An indefatigable and highly methodical worker, Dr. Barrus doubtlessly thought she was forwarding Burroughs' reputation after his death as assiduously and successfully as before it. To some extent, such was the case. The only drawback, so far as Burroughs' reputation and posthumous influence were concerned, was that the public's view of him was controlled more or less exclusively by Clara Barrus' adulatory feelings and opinions, for she exploited to the fullest extent the vast hoard of diaries, notebooks, letters, manuscripts, notes on conversations, and scrapbooks at her disposal, leaving little for more objective scholars to work with. Other books on Burroughs were published during the decade after his death, but they were in the nature of reminiscences and impressions—not in any sense solid biography—until the appearance of Elizabeth Burroughs Kelley's *John Burroughs: Naturalist* in 1959, which is based in part on original papers not available even to Dr. Barrus. One must not, of course, underestimate Dr. Barrus' services. She was an intelligent, enthusiastic, and above all, hard-working woman who gave many years of her life to the literary career of John Burroughs. But, untrained as she was as a critic or scholar, she permitted herself to stray from objectivity in her selection of materials and in her occasional omission of vital phrases and sentences from material that she included in her books.

III *Critical Opinion*

But Burroughs did receive some nonbiographical critical attention after his death despite the inaccessibility of so many of his papers. In

1923, Norman Foerster in his *Nature in American Literature* assessed a number of major nature writers against the humanistic criterion stated by Arnold in lines that form the epigraph of the book: "Know, man hath all that Nature hath, but more,/And in that more lie all his hopes of God." Foerster feels that Burroughs was too much a naturalist, too much a monist unwilling to set man apart from nature, to meet Arnold's standard, but that he had leanings toward a modified form of humanism, and to this extent he met with Foerster's hearty approbation. Foerster's observation is astute. To be a humanist Burroughs would have to believe that man had qualities and potentials not only peculiar to himself but independent of the natural constitution of the universe. Burroughs would not go this far, but he did insist that, within the natural order, man's evolution brought into being such values as a sense of justice, a discrimination between good and evil and between the ugly and the beautiful, and altruistic love, which had hitherto been unknown in nature. With this one reservation Foerster otherwise has little but praise for Burroughs, whom he ranks with Muir as the best prose writer in American literature since Thoreau. Foerster is extremely successful, within the forty pages he gives to the subject, in tracing the influences on Burroughs and his intellectual development as a Transcendentalist coping with scientific naturalism.

In 1924, Philip M. Hicks in a highly competent University of Pennsylvania doctoral dissertation, *The Development of the Natural History Essay in American Literature*, concluded that Burroughs' some three hundred essays on nature subjects rank him first in this genre, with the possible exception only of Thoreau. In Burroughs he sees the culmination of a tradition of American nature writing that had its beginning in the eighteenth century with men like John and William Bartram and St. Jean de Crèvecoeur. The favorable comparison with Thoreau, though surprising perhaps to some, is not unmerited. Lacking the shock effect that titillates so many in Thoreau's writing, Burroughs preached a similar text—that wonder lies all about man and is his for the taking, if only he would wake up to its presence.

As for what the future reputation of Burroughs as a writer will be, the answer may lie with the bird-watchers, the conservationists, and all the growing numbers determined to retain some of North America's natural beauty for their own appreciation and that of later generations. Such persons, of course, have interests which are by no means confined to ornithology or conservation—interests which are amply fed by Burroughs—but which extend to the broader scientific, literary, and theological matters so frequently the subject of his writing. These readers will be drawn to Burroughs for a long time to come, but for their own delight they should become more aware of his writing on other than outdoor subjects. The mistake of ignoring Burroughs' wider experience and preoccupations is emphasized in a 1969 essay by T. Morris Longstreth. Relating how Burroughs was his "first man of letters," whose books he had read in the library of his Quaker school, he describes his initial attraction: "I found in him a fellow enthusiast about our home-known nature. He had put the outdoor things I saw, felt, loved, but only half knew, into convenient little books."[2] Invited as a youth to visit Burroughs, Longstreth, who himself later won a reputation as a nature writer, made the mistake that so many make of not looking a little beneath the more obvious and generally known facets of the experiences of this "quiet explorer" (12) of life. Longstreth had brought his own immediate interests with him to Slabsides, and it did not occur to him that his host could point the way to new ones. Thus, for example, he lost the opportunity of conversing about Whitman with one of the poet's closest friends.

Not only conservationists but students of American literature and of intellectual history would be rewarded if they would read other than Burroughs' admittedly superb outdoor pieces. They would find that Burroughs wrote sensitively, perceptively, and analytically about his total environment—not only the natural beauties and resources that are the American heritage, but the riches of science, literature, philosophy, and moral values that are as much a part of the environment as the seas, the earth, and the skies, and as indispensable to man's survival. What Burroughs has to say about Whitman, Darwin, and Bergson is fully as important as what he has to say about the birds—as countless thoughtful American readers during the sixty years of his literary life were aware.

Notes and References

Page references to the twenty-three books included in the Riverby Edition of John Burroughs' works are to that edition. In the case of books not included in it, references are to the editions listed in the Bibliography of this study.

Chapter One

1. Clara Barrus, *Our Friend John Burroughs* (Boston, 1914), p. 196.
2. Clara Barrus, *The Life and Letters of John Burroughs* (Boston, 1925), I, p. 60.
3. "John Burroughs in His Mountain Hut," *The New Voice*, XVI (August 19, 1899), 7 and 13. The same account, somewhat revised and expanded, may be found in Orison S. Marden, *How They Succeeded: The Life Stories of Successful Men Told By Themselves* (Boston: Lothrop Publishing Company, [1901]). Marden, who edited this book, gives Dreiser no credit for the chapter on Burroughs, though it was obviously closely derived from *The New Voice* article. Marden was editor of *The New Voice* and of a periodical named *Success*, in the September, 1898, issue of which an earlier version of Dreiser's interview appeared.
4. *Ibid.*, p. 7.
5. *Life and Letters*, I, pp. 35-36.
6. *Ibid.*, I, p. 39.
7. Barrus, *Our Friend John Burroughs*, p. 105.
8. *Life and Letters*, I, p. 41.
9. Barrus, *Our Friend John Burroughs*, p. 128.
10. *Life and Letters*, I, pp. 45-46.
11. *The New York Saturday Press*, III (July 21, 1860), 1.
12. Barrus, *Our Friend John Burroughs*, p. 171.
13. Letter from Myron Benton to John Burroughs, August 3, 1862; also quoted in *Life and Letters*, I, p. 63. The correspondence between these two—approximately 150 letters by each, now deposited in the Berg Collection in the New York Public Library—is a major source of insights into Burroughs' intellectual and artistic development.

Chapter Two

1. Clara Barrus, *Whitman and Burroughs Comrades* (Boston, 1931), p. 4.

2. Letter from John Burroughs to Myron Benton, December 19, 1863; also in Clara Barrus, *Whitman and Burroughs Comrades*, p. 13.

3. See also *Whitman and Burroughs Comrades*, p. 24.

4. Gay Wilson Allen, *The Solitary Singer* (New York, 1955), p. 375.

5. *Life and Letters*, I, pp. 116-17.

6. *Notes on Walt Whitman as Poet and Person*, Second Edition (New York, 1871), p. 122. All citations are to the second edition, which is substantially the same as the first, excepting some additional material at the end.

7. Barrus, *Whitman and Burroughs Comrades*, p. 53.

8. *Life and Letters*, I, p. 128.

9. *Ibid.*

10. Barrus, *Whitman and Burroughs Comrades*, p. 51.

11. *Ibid.*

12. References are to the Riverby Edition of *Birds and Poets*, which includes "Before Genius" with, curiously, the allusions to Whitman removed.

13. Barrus, *Whitman and Burroughs Comrades*, p. 127.

14. Clara Barrus (ed.), *The Heart of Burroughs's Journals* (Boston, 1928), p. 69.

15. *Life and Letters*, I, p. 193.

16. Letters of John Burroughs to R. Bucke, January 25, 1880, and June 17, 1881.

17. *The Heart of Burroughs's Journals*, p. 40.

18. *Ibid.*, pp. 41-42.

19. *Life and Letters*, I, p. 192.

20. Letter of John Burroughs to R. Bucke, December 31, 1880.

21. Barrus, *Whitman and Burroughs Comrades*, pp. 299-300.

22. *Dostoyevsky*, translated by Donald Attwater (New York, 1957), p. 227.

23. *John Burroughs and Ludella Peck* (New York, 1925), p. 3.

24. *Ibid.*, p. 4.

25. Barrus, *Whitman and Burroughs Comrades*, p. 299.

26. Fëdor Dostoevski, *The Brothers Karamazov*, translated by Constance Garnett (New York, 1950), p. 127. For further parallels between Whitman and Dostoevski, see P. D. Westbrook, *The Greatness of Man: An Essay on Dostoyevsky and Whitman* (New York, 1961).

27. *Ibid.*

28. Fëdor Dostoevski, *The Possessed*, translated by Constance Garnett (New York, 1936), p. 256.

29. As here, Burroughs frequently quotes inaccurately.

Chapter Three

1. *The Heart of Burroughs's Journals*, p. 88.
2. See H. A. Taine, *History of English Literature*, translated by H. Van Laun (New York, 1879), II, pp. 435ff.
3. J. R. Lowell, *My Study Windows* (Boston, 1890), p. 203.
4. *The Heart of Burroughs's Journals*, pp. 130-31.
5. *Ibid.*, p. 131.
6. *Birds and Bees* (Boston, 1887), p. 4. Mary Burt later edited two collections of Burroughs' writing for Ginn and Company of Boston—entitled *Little Nature Studies for Little People* (Volume I, 1895; Volume II, 1896)—as second and third readers.
7. *Life and Letters*, I, p. 285.

Chapter Four

1. Barrus, *Our Friend John Burroughs*, p. 108.
2. *Life and Letters*, I, p. 75.
3. *Ibid.*, I, p. 146.
4. *Ibid.*
5. *Ibid.*, I, p. 145.
6. See Henry James, *Views and Reviews* (Freeport, New York: 1968), pp. 217-18.
7. Letter of John Burroughs to Orlando Rouland, January 11, 1911.
8. *Life and Letters*, II, p. 119.
9. *Ibid.*, II, p. 122.

Chapter Five

1. Letter of John Burroughs to Myron Benton, September 24, 1876.
2. *The Heart of Burroughs's Journals*, pp. 97-98.
3. *Ibid.*, p. 98.
4. *Under the Apple-Trees*, p. 185; also paraphrased in *The Breath of Life*, p. 231.
5. Letter of John Burroughs to Myron Benton, January 20, 1894.
6. *The Heart of Burroughs's Journals*, p. 333.
7. Letter of John Burroughs to Myron Benton, January 14, 1893.
8. *Ibid.*, November 6, 1893.
9. Charles H. Foster (ed.), *Beyond Concord: Selected Writings of David Atwood Wasson* (Bloomington, Indiana, 1965), p. 131.
10. *The Conduct of Life* (Boston, 1904), p. 27.
11. *Ibid.*, p. 42.
12. *The Light of Day*, p. v.
13. *The Heart of Burroughs's Journals*, p. 205.
14. Letter of John Burroughs to A. B. Paine, January 24, 1913.

Chapter Six

1. *Life and Letters*, I, p. 55.
2. "That Lasts!" *The Christian Science Monitor* (May 1, 1969), p. 12. Robert Henry Welker in *Birds and Men* (Cambridge, Massachusetts, 1955) also strongly urges that Burroughs' philosophical and critical writing be given the attention that it formerly enjoyed.

Selected Bibliography

PRIMARY SOURCES

1. Books (chronologically listed)

Notes on Walt Whitman as Poet and Person. New York: American News Company, 1867.

Wake-Robin. New York: Hurd and Houghton, 1871.

Winter Sunshine. New York: Hurd and Houghton, 1875.

Birds and Poets with Other Papers. New York: Hurd and Houghton, 1877.

Locusts and Wild Honey. Boston: Houghton, Osgood and Company, 1879.

Pepacton. Boston: Houghton Mifflin and Company, 1881.

Fresh Fields. Boston: Houghton Mifflin and Company, 1884.

Signs and Seasons. Boston: Houghton Mifflin and Company, 1886.

Indoor Studies. Boston: Houghton Mifflin and Company, 1889.

Riverby. Boston: Houghton Mifflin and Company, 1894.

Whitman: A Study. Boston: Houghton Mifflin and Company, 1896.

The Light of Day. Boston: Houghton Mifflin and Company, 1900.

John James Audubon. Boston: Small, Maynard and Company, 1902.

Literary Values and Other Papers. Boston: Houghton Mifflin and Company, 1902.

Far and Near. Boston: Houghton Mifflin and Company, 1904.

Ways of Nature. Boston: Houghton Mifflin and Company, 1905.

Bird and Bough. Boston: Houghton Mifflin and Company, 1906.

Camping with President Roosevelt. Boston: Houghton Mifflin and Company, 1906. Reprinted, 1907, as *Camping and Tramping with Roosevelt*, with an additional chapter.

Leaf and Tendril. Boston: Houghton Mifflin and Company, 1908.

Time and Change. Boston: Houghton Mifflin Company, 1912.

The Summit of the Years. Boston: Houghton Mifflin Company, 1913.

The Breath of Life. Boston: Houghton Mifflin Company, 1915.

Under the Apple-Trees. Boston: Houghton Mifflin Company, 1916.

Field and Study. Boston: Houghton Mifflin Company, 1919.

Accepting the Universe. Boston: Houghton Mifflin Company, 1920.
Under the Maples. Boston: Houghton Mifflin Company, 1921.
The Last Harvest. Boston: Houghton Mifflin Company, 1922.
My Boyhood, With a Conclusion by Julian Burroughs. Garden City,
     New York: Doubleday, Page and Company, 1922.
John Burroughs and Ludella Peck. New York: Harold Vinal, 1925,
     Letters.
The Heart of Burroughs's Journals. Edited by Clara Barrus. Boston:
     Houghton Mifflin Company, 1928.

2. Selections
     The books listed below consist of pieces selected from Burroughs'
previously published books and are designed either as school texts or
for the general reader. Not all such volumes are listed here.
Birds and Bees. Introduction by Mary E. Burt. Boston: Houghton
     Mifflin and Company, 1887.
Sharp Eyes and Other Papers. Boston: Houghton Mifflin and Company,
     1888.
A Bunch of Herbs and Other Papers. Boston: Houghton Mifflin and
     Company, [1896].
A Year in the Fields. Introduction and photographs by Clifton
     Johnson. Boston: Houghton Mifflin and Company, 1896.
Squirrels and Other Fur-Bearers. Boston: Houghton Mifflin and
     Company, 1900. (Some simplification and rewriting of originals.)
In the Catskills. Edited with photographs by Clifton Johnson. Boston:
     Houghton Mifflin Company, 1910.
*John Burroughs at Troutbeck: Being Extracts from His Writings
     Published and Unpublished.* Introduction by Vachel Lindsay.
     Troutbeck Leaflets, Number Ten, compiled by J. E. Spingarn.
     Amenia, New York: Troutbeck Press, 1926.
John Burroughs' America. Edited by Farida Wiley. Foreword by Julian
     Burroughs. New York: The Devin-Adair Company, 1951.
With John Burroughs in Field and Wood. Edited and illustrated by
     Elizabeth Burroughs Kelley. South Brunswick, N.J., and New
     York: A. S. Barnes and Company, 1969.

3. Collected Sets
The Riverside (Uniform) Edition. Twenty-three volumes, which include
     all books through *The Last Harvest* in List 1 above, with the
     exception of *Notes on Walt Whitman. . . , John James Audubon,
     Bird and Bough*, and *Camping with President Roosevelt* and its
     sequel. Volume I appeared in 1895; later volumes were added as
     published.

Riverby Edition. Contains same volumes as above. Was published 1904
as limited Autograph Edition. All volumes of the Riverside and
Riverby Editions from *Far and Near* (1904) onward were printed
from the same plates. In addition to being superior in binding and
paper, the Riverby Edition contains illustrations. The Riverby
Edition was reissued (as the Wake-Robin Edition) by William H.
Wise and Company, New York, 1924, and by Russell and Russell,
New York, 1968.

4. Uncollected Essays, Articles, and Introductions
    Most of John Burroughs' essays and other short pieces have been
collected in the regular editions of his works. The list that follows
includes items not found in any of his books but of importance either
in his early development or in their presentation of ideas. I regret that
the apparent nonexistence of files of the New York *Leader* during the
years 1860-62 has made it impossible to list his contributions to it, as
I have done with those to the *Saturday Press*.
"Deep," *New York Saturday Press*, III (May 5, 1860), 2.
"Fragments from the Table of an Intellectual Epicure," *New York
        Saturday Press*, III (May 26, June 9, June 23, June 30, July 7,
        1860), 1, 3, 3, 1, 2.
"A Thought on Culture," *New York Saturday Press*, III (July 21,
        1860), 1.
"Poetry," *New York Saturday Press*, III (November 3, 1860), 3.
"Expression," *Atlantic Monthly*, VI (November, 1860), 572-77.
"Analogy," *Knickerbocker*, LX (December, 1862), 477-84.
"Walt Whitman and His 'Drum Taps,' " *Galaxy*, II (December 1, 1866),
        606-15. Reused in part in *Notes on Walt Whitman as Poet and
        Person* (1867) and in *Whitman: A Study* (1896).
"Walt Whitman and His Recent Critics," *In Re Walt Whitman*. Ed.
        Horace Traubel *et al.* Philadelphia: David McKay, 1893, pp.
        93-108.
"Walt Whitman and the Common People," in *In Re Walt Whitman*, pp.
        363-65.
"The Poet and the Modern," *Atlantic Monthly*, LXXVIII (October,
        1896), 565-66.
"Introduction," *Songs of Nature*. Ed. John Burroughs. New York:
        McClure Phillips and Company, 1901, pp. v-x.
"Walt Whitman," *Encyclopaedia Britannica*, 10th ed. (1902), XXIII,
        840-41; 11th ed. (1911), XXVIII, 610-11.
"Real and Sham Natural History," *Atlantic Monthly*, XCI (March,
        1903), 298-309.
"Burns, the Glorious Sinner," An Unpublished Essay by John Bur-
        roughs, *Boston Public Library Quarterly*, XI (October, 1959),
        193-99.

SECONDARY SOURCES

1. Bibliographies

BLANCK, J. N. "John Burroughs." *Bibliography of American Literature*, I. New Haven: Yale University Press, 1955, pp. 433-48. A complete listing of books, items published as parts of books, collections, collected editions, and volumes about Burroughs.

GARRISON, JOSEPH M., JR. "John Burroughs." *Bulletin of Bibliography*, XXIV (May and August, 1964), 95, 96, 94. A subtitle accurately describes this valuable work: *A Checklist of Published Literary Criticism Including Essays on Natural History Containing Literary Criticism or Comment.*

2. Biographical and Critical

Both as a naturalist and as a literary figure John Burroughs has received widespread attention. The following list attempts to be representative as well as selective. Standard references such as biographical dictionaries and literary histories have not been included. Biographies and studies of Walt Whitman usually give considerable attention to Burroughs.

BARRUS, CLARA. *John Burroughs Boy and Man.* Garden City, New York: Doubleday, Page and Company, 1920. Originally designed as a book for young people, but of interest to mature readers. Contains a number of Burroughs' letters. Especially useful in regard to his relationship with E. M. Allen, who introduced him to Whitman.

———. *The Life and Letters of John Burroughs, Two Volumes.* Boston: Houghton Mifflin Company, 1925. Most comprehensive biography thus far, containing numerous letters and quotations from diaries, notebooks, and other manuscripts.

———. *Our Friend John Burroughs.* Boston: Houghton Mifflin Company, 1914. Includes over a hundred pages of "Autobiographical Sketches" by Burroughs.

———. *Whitman and Burroughs Comrades.* Boston: Houghton Mifflin Company, 1931. Detailed, thorough coverage of the Burroughs-Whitman friendship; contains many letters, parts of unpublished manuscripts, and obscure published material.

BENTON, JOEL. "John Burroughs," *Scribner's Monthly*, XIII (January, 1877), pp. 336-41. First important critical essay on Burroughs.

DREISER, THEODORE. "John Burroughs in His Mountain Hut," *The New Voice*, XVI (August 19, 1899), 7 and 13. Fascinating attempt to present Burroughs' character and way of life.

DE LOACH, R. J. H. *Rambles with John Burroughs.* Boston: The Gorham Press, 1912. Interesting personalia.

FOERSTER, NORMAN. *Nature in American Literature.* New York:

Russell and Russell, 1958 (first published in 1923). The chapter on Burroughs is the most scholarly and methodical consideration of Burroughs' significance thus far to appear.

FRISBEE, LUCY. *John Burroughs: Boy of Field and Stream.* Indianapolis: The Bobbs-Merrill Company, 1964. Part of the "Childhood of Famous Americans" series, this book exemplifies Burroughs' continuing reputation as an American folk hero.

GARLAND, HAMLIN. *Afternoon Neighbors.* New York: The Macmillan Company, 1934. Reminiscences, anecdotes, and factual information from a close friend of Burroughs in his later years.

———. *Roadside Meetings.* New York: The Macmillan Company, 1930. Reminiscences about Burroughs.

HARING, H. A. Editor, *The Slabsides Book of John Burroughs.* Boston: Houghton Mifflin Company, 1931. Personal impressions of Burroughs by a number of his friends.

HICKS, PHILIP M. *The Development of the Natural History Essay in American Literature.* Philadelphia: University of Pennsylvania Press, 1924. Places Burroughs' nature essays in the context of the genre as developed in the United States.

HUBBARD, ELBERT (under pseudonym Fra Elbertus). *Old John Burroughs.* East Aurora, New York, The Roycroft Shop [1901]. Charming, perceptive evaluation of character.

JAMES, HENRY. *Views and Reviews.* Freeport, New York: Books for Libraries Press, [1968]. Appreciative, sensitive criticism of Burroughs' *Winter Sunshine.*

JOHNSON, CLIFTON. *John Burroughs Talks: His Reminiscences and Comments.* Boston: Houghton Mifflin Company, 1922. Reports of conversations with Burroughs on many subjects.

KELLEY, ELIZABETH BURROUGHS. *John Burroughs: Naturalist, the Story of His Work and Family.* New York: Exposition Press, 1959. Mrs. Kelley, Burroughs' granddaughter, draws upon hitherto untapped manuscript sources as well as on family memories and tradition to present a fresh, revealing, and understanding portrait of her grandfather as well as of her father, Julian Burroughs.

KENNEDY, W. S. *The Real John Burroughs.* New York: Funk and Wagnalls Company, 1924. Somewhat sensational and sentimental; not totally to be relied on, but containing some insights.

PERRY, BLISS. *The Praise of Folly and Other Papers.* Boston: Houghton Mifflin Company, 1923. The essay "John Burroughs" (pp. 63-72) is well considered, fair, and perceptive.

OSBORN, H. F. *Impressions of Great Naturalists.* New York: Charles Scribner's Sons, 1924. In the chapter "The Two Johns" Osborn compares Burroughs and John Muir as to race and temperament.

OSBORNE, CLIFFORD H. *The Religion of John Burroughs.* Boston: Houghton Mifflin Company, 1930. Highly competent summary of Burroughs' religious and philosophical ideas.

SHARP, D. L. "Fifty Years of John Burroughs," *Atlantic Monthly*, CVI (November, 1910), 631-41. One of the most favorable critiques ever written on Burroughs. Ranks him among the greatest of nature writers.

————. *The Seer of Slabsides.* Boston: Houghton Mifflin Company, 1921. Contains the essay listed immediately above as well as others.

WELKER, ROBERT HENRY. *Birds and Men: American Birds in Science, Art, Literature, and Conservation, 1800-1900.* Cambridge: The Belknap Press of Harvard University Press, 1955. Very strong on the literary naturalists, among whom Burroughs (treated in Chapter 9, "John O' Birds: John Burroughs," pp. 125-35) is placed high both as a scientist and a writer. Pleads for attention to Burroughs as a philosopher and especially as a literary critic.

WESTBROOK, PERRY. "John Burroughs and the Transcendentalists," *Emerson Society Quarterly*, No. 55, Part Two (Second Quarter, 1969), pp. 47-55. Survey of Burroughs' critical essays on Emerson, Thoreau, and Whitman.

Index